The Horse
Its Action and Anatomy

THE HORSE

Its Action and Anatomy
by an Artist

LOWES DALBIAC LUARD

J. A. ALLEN   LONDON

Second, paperback edition published in Great Britain by
J.A. Allen & Co. Ltd
1 Lower Grosvenor Place
London SW1W 0EL
1996

Originally published in 1935 by Faber and Faber Ltd, London
and reprinted in 1956

British Library Cataloguing in Publication Data
A catalogue record for this title is available from the
British Library.

ISBN 0 85131 645 X

Colour reproduction by Tenon and Polert (Hong Kong)
Printed and bound by Dah Hua (Hong Kong)

Contents

Foreword by the
RT HON. Sir Nicholas Lyell, QC, MP

Observation, emotional response and analysis – Luard's art was a combination of all three. What thrilled him was movement and muscular power. But he also wished to understand. So behind his work, which was influenced in his youth by a combination of the Barbizon and the Bande Noir, by Jean François Millet from a generation earlier and his own tutors in France, Lucien Simon and René Ménard at La Grande Chaumière, lay a deep desire to master the fundamentals.

Luard trained at the Slade. He was a contemporary of Ambrose McEvoy and Augustus John. He spent his early years in England earning his living in London, painting portraits and illustrating. Then in 1904 he went to Paris with his wife Louie and their baby daughter Veronica (my mother) to study in Paris. He intended to stay there three months. They stayed twenty-five years. He was fascinated and inspired by the Percheron carthorses that were everywhere to be seen; the only nude, he said, that could be observed at work.

Luard's most powerful period was from about 1908 to the outbreak of the First World War. His large drawings and pastels have immense power. In August 1914 he joined the Army Service Corps as a Second Lieutenant at the age of forty-two. In a sense it was a tragedy that he was not a war artist. There can have been no artist whose style and temperament were more suited to the capture of the heroic and terrifying effort contributed to that dreadful conflict by the horse.

To depict that movement and muscular power the first essential was to train the memory. This skill Luard underpinned with his

ix

Foreword

study of the photographs of Edward Muybridge and his own translation of the work of the great French teacher Lecoq de Boisbaudron entitled *The Training of the Memory in Art.*

After the War the family returned to their flat and he to his studio in the 14th Arrondissement of Paris. For a while his drawing and painting took on a calmer and more reposed character – a reaction perhaps to the effort and struggle of the War. It was then that Luard gave his attention to the preparation and production of this book, studying the anatomy of the horse, whose action he already understood so well, first at the French government veterinary school at Alfort near Paris and then, after his return to England in 1930, at the Royal Veterinary College.

His book is the first and fullest study of the skeleton, muscles and physiognomy of the horse since Stubbs. It has for sixty years been consulted not only by artists but by veterinarians and chiropractors. This new edition, which, thanks to the veterinary expertise of Peter Gray, includes revisions which reflect our current state of knowledge and terminology, will I hope be of value to both artists and veterinarians for generations to come.

Author's Preface

Should an artist learn anatomy? is a question still undecided. The Greek sculptors, we are told, acquired their knowledge of the construction of the body merely through the daily observation of naked athletes; whereas Leonardo da Vinci and Dürer, artists with a strong scientific bent, studied anatomy.

But anatomical study is scientific, and science, in the opinion of a certain school of thought, has nothing to do with art.

Difficult questions these, for artists get results acknowledged by real judges as true art, by methods strangely opposite. Does not the least scientific of artists or poets transmute and embody in his art or poetry a mass of practical knowledge acquired in daily living? Cannot then knowledge deliberately acquired be similarly transmuted?

While it is for you, reader, to decide if anatomy will help or hurt you as an artist, I offer you this reflection that, whereas any ignorance may be repaired by well-directed study, there is no process, I know of, by which particular knowledge can be discarded at will.

The plates in this book are based upon drawings made in the dissecting theatre and the museum of the French Government Veterinary School at Alfort, near Paris, where I was given every facility for study.

In London, I have been allowed by the courtesy of Sir Frederick Hobday to come for help and advice to the Royal Veterinary College; and I have particularly to thank Mr. C. W. Ottaway for his kindness. He not only put his knowledge at my disposal, but found time to

Author's Preface

read my proofs and save me from those errors which a layman is so certain of committing.

My thanks are also due to the Royal College of Veterinary Surgeons for allowing me to make a liberal use of the books in their library.

Preface to Second Edition
by Peter Gray, MVB, MRCVS

The quality of this remarkable book, *The Horse – Its Action and Anatomy, by an Artist* is best appreciated by comparing the anatomical detail it contains with that available in the latest texts around today. It is the work of an artist who could not only depict a horse in flowing movement but who also had an outstanding knowledge of its anatomy. Diagrams such as Plate 11 describe in perfect detail the structures involved in the main stay apparatus of both fore and hind limbs. They are accurate in detail and in description.

However, changes have occurred since the writing of the first edition. These amount, mainly, to differences in classification, based on a need for greater uniformity, in both common and scientific names. Some changes are matters of style only: the dropping of hyphens, the joining of words. There are also changes in terminology and nomenclature which have been necessitated by this same classifying process. Thus 'lateral' and 'medial' have replaced 'external' and 'internal'; 'cranial' and 'caudal' have replaced 'anterior' and 'posterior'; 'dorsal' and 'ventral' have replaced 'upper' and 'lower'. The word 'volar' is also sometimes used, indicating the sole or palm, used for the flexor surface of the limb, as opposed to the extensor surface, which might be 'dorsal' in the same context.

In a similar way, names such as 'perforans' and 'perforatus', formerly in everyday use – referring to muscles and their tendons in the limbs – have been abandoned for 'superficial' and 'deep flexor', an instance of change that is both pragmatic and simple when we speak about the same tendons and their relative positions at the back of the leg.

Preface to Second Edition

As examples of what is meant generally take the following from the Descriptive List of Muscles, Chapter IV (page 55):

2. Levator of the Upper Lip and Nostril *(L. nasi Labialis)*.
The common name for this muscle is now levator nasolabialis *(m. nasolabialis)*, the scientific name being given in parenthesis.

25a. Serratus Posterior *(S. Exspiratorius)*.
This is now named the serratus caudalis *(m. serratus dorsalis caudalis)*. In this case there is a fundamental change in classification indicated by the new scientific name, showing the position of the muscle relative to other structures.

The original work has been fully preserved and no changes have been made to text or diagrams. However, in an effort to inform the reader of changes in physiological understanding an Addenda has been added at the end of the book. For example, as an addendum to Chapter IV - The Muscles, a list is provided of the current name in use for each muscle mentioned in the author's descriptive list. This is set out as above, with the common name first and the scientific name following, in brackets.

Finally, it is necessary to say that this work amounted to an excellent achievement for anyone whose career was not in professional equine anatomy. Its quality, even today, is one of which any professional anatomist could be proud. Lowes Dalbiac Luard may well have been an artist by inclination; he could also have described himself as an equine anatomist based on the complexity of his understanding and the quality of his diagrams in this book.

Illustrations

Coloured Plates

The Skeleton

For clearness' sake the Skeleton is shown with only one fore leg and one hind leg. Distributed through the book are illustrations of bones and joints drawn from various points of view, which the reader should compare with this Plate.

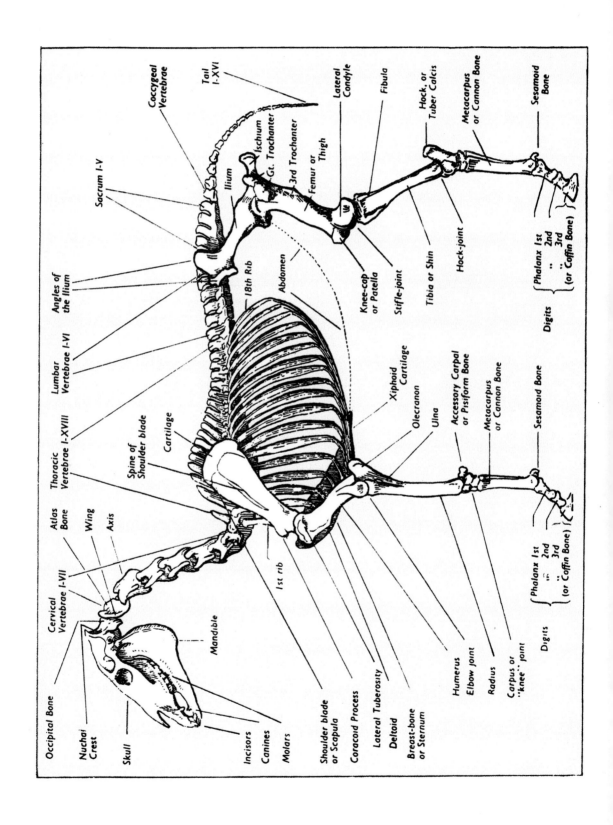

Chapter I. The Frame

As the only purpose of an artistic anatomy is to help the artist in the observation of form, it can neglect the intricacies of nerves, veins, arteries and many other organs to concern itself almost exclusively with the bones and muscles—one might say the superficial muscles, if it were not that occasionally muscles that are completely hidden should be studied, because an understanding of their action leads to the better understanding of the action of the muscles that show.

Thus limited, the study of what we may call the mechanical anatomy of the horse is comparatively simple, the more so that a horse can do so few things. Outcry from some reader at this aspersion on a noble animal!

The horse excels indeed in trotting, galloping, jumping, pulling weights and carrying loads; a true title to nobility, for such powers serve the convenience and pleasure of man. Its strength and endurance are prodigious. It can lift itself with the added weight of a rider over a jump and recover safely on landing, and even when mounted can gallop down a free running deer.

But to achieve such amazing feats it needs to be made rather rigid. Consequently though it goes forward so brilliantly it goes backwards moderately, lies down and gets up awkwardly, and generally has to make several clumsy efforts before it can roll over on its back. And this necessary rigidity of its backbone and other parts limits the variety of its possible attitudes, and reduces its scope as a subject for the draughtsman. Think of the bending and twisting powers of a cat.

1

The Bones   Let us begin our study by looking at the bones, and try to see what is required of the muscles to make them act. Bones and

muscles are, of course, inter-dependent, the bones deciding as it were the points of attachment of the muscles and the directions in which they are to pull; being moulded in their turn by the requirements of the muscles, with twists and channels and knobs, that the muscles may get their required purchase and be able to do their work without interfering with each other.

Look first at that essential principle in the construction of all quadrupeds, the difference in the way in which the body is supported by the fore and hind legs.

Support of the Body   The support of the body by the hind legs is through the direct contact of bone with bone, the head of the femur being fitted into the socket of the pelvis, whereas in front the body

is slung, being supported from the underside of the shoulder blade by muscles and tendons attached to the ribs (see skeleton, Frontispiece, and Pl. 5, p. 58).

Such differences in construction are adapted to the special duties of the fore and hind quarters. Thus the force of the hind legs, the chief engines of propulsion, is transmitted without loss through the direct thrust of bone on bone, and the fore legs are able to take up without shock the momentum of horse and rider alighting

over a jump because the body is attached to them by slings. *Support of*
It may be objected that a man alights upon legs which are *the Body*
fitted directly into the socket of his pelvis and yet jumps without injury. But the comparison is not quite fair; for his legs
both propel and catch him and so are not asked to catch more
than they themselves have lifted, as the horse's fore legs are.
For a horse's hind legs have a power which far exceeds that of
the fore legs, galloping, jumping, pulling depending chiefly
upon their action. A comparison of the masses of muscle that
work the hind and fore legs makes this clear.

Another notable difference of structure is in the feet. The *The Feet*
fore legs have hoofs which are larger and rounder than those
of the hind feet, being designed to carry more
weight, for they have to support the weight of
the head and neck in addition to their share of
the weight of the body; and the hind feet are
narrower and more pointed, the better to grip
the ground when galloping and jumping. The
front feet too have a wider stance.[1]

Despite the differences, there is a correspondence between the fore and hind legs both *Correspond-*
in construction and in action (see skeleton, *ence of Fore*
Frontispiece, and Pl. 11, p. 108). The shoulder *and Hind*
blade, which transmits the propulsion of the *Limbs*
fore limb to the body, slopes forwards and
downwards to its junction with the upper arm,
as the femur, which conveys the propulsion of the hind limb,
does to its junction with the tibia at the stifle joint; the upper
arm slopes backwards to the elbow, the 'hock' of the fore limb,
as the tibia does to the hock; from which points the legs de-
scend similarly to the pastern and hoof, the hind leg directly,
the fore legs with an added joint, the 'knee'.[2] But the knee

[1]See Chap. IX, p. 104.

[2]Properly the carpus=wrist. The familiar term 'knee' is not fortunate, as the
joint really corresponds to the human wrist.

Correspond-
ence of Fore
and Hind
Limbs

makes no difference in ordinary paces between the propulsive action of the fore leg and that of the hind leg, as it is maintained unbent; it is in the advancement of the fore leg that the use of the knee comes in, to lift the foot clear of the ground to prevent tripping, and to raise it well out of the way as when jumping.

In a quiet pace such as the walk, the fore and hind legs behave very similarly, serving much like the spoke of a wheel. It is only in violent movements such as galloping and jumping that their differences of action really come out and the purpose of their differences of structure becomes clear.

Often in books of artistic anatomy little or no attempt is made to study the effect of the action and interplay of the different parts, the muscles being merely mapped as flexors and extensors, that is, muscles that close a joint or pull it open. Such classifications, necessary as they are, should be supplemented with some explanation of the movements resulting from the action of muscles when working in combination. And this can best be done, I think, by trying to work out how some particular action is effected.

Action of
Muscles

Let us think then not of how a horse shoots his foot backwards as in kicking, but of how from the resistance of the

stationary hoof on the ground these same muscles of his leg are used to push him forwards. To think always of his movements in this way is to get, I believe, a better understanding of a horse's action, a better 'feel' of the forces and stresses which create the sequence of shapes and rhythms that the artist enjoys. Let us approach the study of the muscles as an inventor's problem of how best to operate the given levers, the bones, so as to supply the required momentum to the body. Study the skeleton and before you look at the diagrams of the muscles ask yourself what muscles you would design, and you will, I am sure, understand better nature's solution of the problem.

But before studying the muscles, which are reserved for another chapter, let us continue our general survey of the skeleton (see the Frontispiece).

Look at the vertebral column and for the moment that part of it from the hips to the chest which forms the back. The

vertebral column, which runs from the head to the tip of the tail, is composed of a series of bones connected by joints, which vary enormously in their construction and their flexibility, the neck bones being deeply embedded one in the other, with ball - and - socket joints, whereas the tail bones are really not socketed into each other at all. This gives such flexibility to the tail that a horse can swish it up and down, sideways or round and round with absolute freedom; and the deep ball and socketing of the neck bones allows for the pull of strong muscles without any danger of dislocation. In the backbone the vertebræ are firmly connected without much play, so that it may be a firm though not rigid column.

The horse's power of carrying weight depends upon this firm knitting of the bones of the back, to which the slight arching of it contributes. The backbone runs up to the pelvis from a point in the middle of the chest where the neck properly begins. And the height of the withers, so

The Frame

The Vertebral Column characteristic of the shape of a horse, is, we see, not directly due to the backbone, but to the long processes which stand up from it.

The variation in the processes on the different vertebræ is very striking. They are, of course, modified to suit their duties. The long processes that form the withers serve to support the neck and head, and are raked backwards the better to resist this pull. On the loins the upright processes are

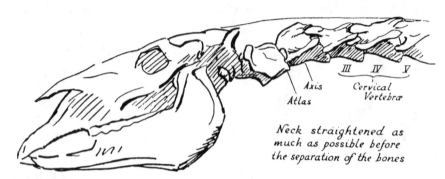

Axis
Atlas
III IV V
Cervical Vertebra

Neck straightened as much as possible before the separation of the bones

shorter and blunter (it is the only comfortable place to sit on a bare-backed donkey, with its knife-edged backbone), and are inclined slightly forward: and the transverse processes are very strongly developed into broad flat blades, for the attachment of strong muscles (see illustration, p. 33). Where the pelvis is attached, a section of the backbone is actually rigid, for the vertebræ are welded into a solid mass, called the sacrum; and the sacrum, making a unit with the pelvis, transmits the drive of the hind legs to the body.

The Neck The neck is not equally flexible in all directions. It moves freely downwards, upwards to a certain height, but not very freely sideways; for the deep entry of the ball of one vertebra into the socket of its neighbour and the large development of their transverse processes check the lateral movement. The two points of its greatest flexibility are near the chest and just behind the head. There the skull is supported by the atlas bone on which it has an up-and-down movement only, the

atlas being able to rotate upon the axis bone through about *The Neck*
three-quarters of a circle. The flanges on the atlas, necessarily
strongly developed for the attachment of the strong muscles
that support the head, are very
noticeable in the living animal,
being indeed the only bone the
forms of which show on the surface between the head and the
chest.

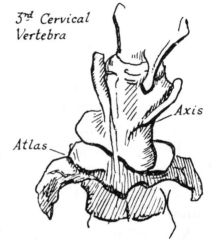

In the skull itself a striking *The Skull*
characteristic is the enormous
depth of the jaw and maxilla
to give the molar teeth deep
secure sockets, and the marked
ridges of bone on the side of
the face for the attachment of

*Atlas turned as far as possible
on the axis; seen from underneath*

the strong Masseter muscles that
work it. In a dead horse, or one that is lying down, the head
looks almost too large and too heavy to be lifted. It is, however,
lighter than it looks, for the skull contains immense hollow
chambers, the sinuses, which communicate with the nasal
cavity.

The horse has eighteen ribs on each side, of which the *The Ribs*
strongest are at the chest where they are attached firmly to
the breast bone, the first
eight ribs receiving the
insertions of the branches
of the big Serratus mus-
cle (39*b*) upon which the
weight of the body is
carried from the shoulder
blade. Towards the quar-
ters the ribs are inclined backwards and are thinner and more
mobile, allowing play to the lungs and other internal organs.

The Shoulder Blades   A horse has no collar bones, as we have, because they would not serve him. Our shoulder blades are on our flat back and our collar bones keep our arms apart that we may the better use them. A horse is flattened laterally and his shoulder blades, which lie along his chest, move freely forwards and backwards at every stride. If you will look at his skeleton from in front (see illustration, p. 27), you will see that his chest is boat-shaped, so that his shoulder blade in moving forward comes nearer to and brings his foot nearer to the central line of his motion.

There are many constructions and adaptations of shape in the bones, on which I have not touched, to which reference will be made later when treating of the muscles and their action.

And now let us turn from the skeleton to the muscles that work it.

Chapter II. Action and Mechanics

I suggested that the best way for the reader to understand the muscles and their action would be to study the bones, and try to invent some of the required muscles for himself. A difficult task, for a horse, like any living thing, is of an intricacy beyond the most ingenious machine ever invented by man. Man indeed has only surpassed the animals in speed and power by limiting each machine to some special purpose, and he has been anticipated in all his inventions by nature—at least it is difficult to think of anything that he has done the principle of which is not embodied in some creature. There is the eel that stuns with an electrical discharge: creatures in the darkness of the deep sea that light their way with head lamps like a car: the little Indian fish that can shoot at a distance of six feet the insects that flutter overhead with a jet of water, as the naturalist shoots humming birds: there is a fish too that has a rod and line with hooks, with which he grapples and stroke-hauls his prey: in the eye there is a muscle that changes the direction of its pull by working through a ring as its pulley: the bird's wing is both plane and propeller; and the aeroplane that does not lift its wheels and carriage wears 'trousers', to break the air resistance, as the eagle wears feathers on his legs: and the horse's leg, when on the ground, works like

Chatodon Rostratus

9

the spoke of a wheel—which brings us back to our sub-ject.

In our study of the muscles let us begin with the legs, as we did in studying the bones. When a horse is standing still, as in stable, he remains planted firmly on both his fore legs for a long time without altering his position, but is continually

shifting the weight of his quarters from one hind leg to the other. The reason for this is that his forehand is entirely sup-ported by inelastic[1] tissues, whereas his quarters are supported partly by muscular force, so that he is compelled frequently to change his position to rest his muscles. If a horse does not stand planted equally on both fore feet, but eases one of them, it is a sure sign that he has some soreness or inflammation in the limb.

The weight of the fore part of the body is supported from the underside of the shoulder blade by the great Serratus

---

[1] 'Inelastic'. The word must not be taken literally, as it is applied for convenience of explanation to tissues that, though not truly inelastic, reach a point at which they are not further extensible.

Thoracis muscle (39*b*), the eight branches of which are attached to the first eight ribs (see Pls. 2, 5 and 11).

The middle branches of
the muscle are interspersed
with inelastic fibres which,
when the muscle is relaxed,
support the body without
any fatigue to the horse.
The weight of the body pulling on the shoulder blade
tends to flex, to close, the

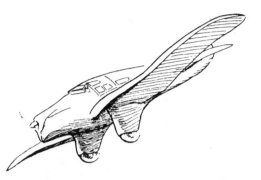

joint at A (Pl. 11, p. 108), so here also there is an arrangement
of inelastic tissue to keep the joint from closing. The Biceps
Brachii muscle (47), which is attached to the shoulder blade at
one end and, passing over the humerus, is attached to the
radius at the other, could do this work and often does, for it is
the extensor of the joint, but it would become exhausted if it
had to support the horse all the time, and so it is relieved of
this duty by the inelastic tissue which forms part of it.

The only possibility now of the horse collapsing is if his
knee, C, were to buckle forward, so another inelastic string
is inserted at a point on the cannon bone below the knee. A
strong tendinous band, found in the External Radial Extensor
(53), it is attached at its upper end to the Biceps muscle (47),
so that it is drawn the tighter, the more the latter tightens.

In Pl. 11 the construction is depicted diagrammatically with
coloured lines, the Biceps green, the External Radial Extensor mauve, which make it clear, I think, that the cord to
below the knee is not only useful for the purpose which has
been described, but is indispensable in violent movements
such as landing over a jump. For then the greater the pull of
the body upon the shoulder blade the greater the tension of
this cord and the more firmly the knee is closed against any
possibility of buckling over.

c   L.T.H.

Plate 1. Bones and Muscles of the Head and Neck

[*The numbers printed after the names of muscles are the numbers of the other plates in which the muscles appear. The plates in which the muscles are best shown are numbered in heavier type.*]

Numbers and Colours of the Muscles

1. Blue — Orbicular muscle of the mouth.
2. Red — Levator of the upper lip and nostril.
3. Mauve — Levator of the upper lip.
4. Green — Zygomaticus.
5. Red — Depressor of the lower lip.
6. Mauve — Buccinator.
7. Yellow — Masseter.
8. Yellow — Lateral dilator of the nose.
9. Green — Superior Dilator of the nose.
10. Yellow — Transverse Dilator of the nose.
11. Buff — Cervical Ligament. Pl. 2.
12. Yellow — Sterno-cephalicus. Pl. 2, 3, 10.
13. Blue — Longus colli (first to seventh cervical vertebræ) attachments.
14. Green — Intertransversales colli (second to seventh cervical vertebræ).

Numbers and Colours of the Muscles

15b. Mauve — Omohyoideus. Pl. 2, 3, 10.
17. Yellow — Rectus capitis. Pl. 2.
18a. Blue — Trapezius, cervical part. Pl. 3, 4, 5.
19. Yellow — Splenius. Pl. 3, 10.
21. Red — Complexus. Pl. 2.
23. Mauve — Posterior Oblique of the head. Pl. 2.
24. Green — Anterior Oblique of the head.
34. Red — Mastoido-Humeralis. Pl. 3, 4, 5, 10.
39a. Mauve — Serratus Cervicis. Pl. 2, 3, 4, 5.
90. { Mauve — Abductor of the ear.
{ Red — External Adductor of the ear.
{ Yellow — Common muscle of the ear.
{ Green — Depressor of the ear.
{ Blue — Levator of the ear.
92a. Blue — Facial vein.
92b. Blue — Jugular vein. Pl. 2, 3, 10.

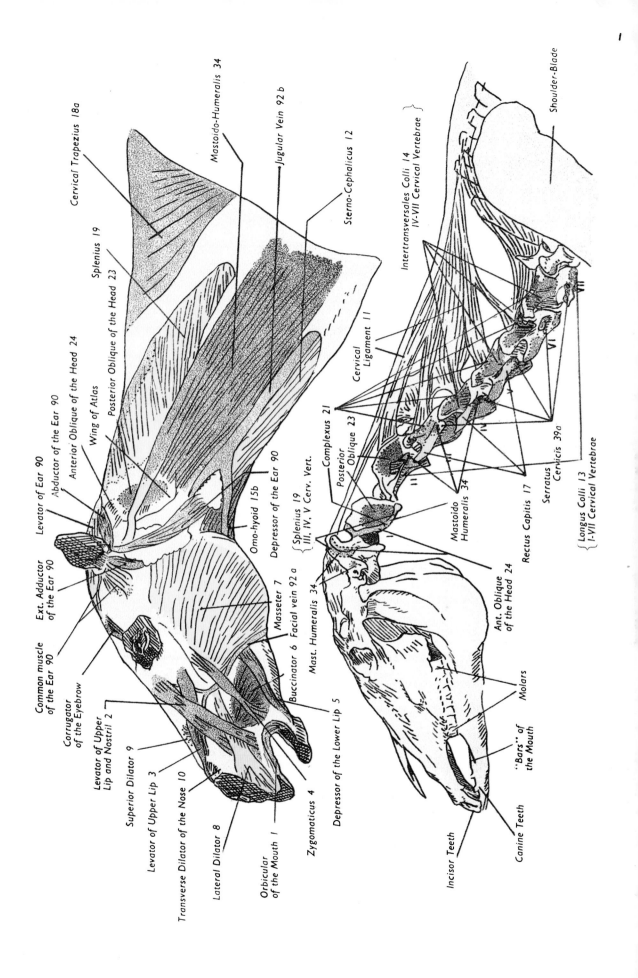

Common muscle
of the Ear 90

Corrugator
of the Eyebrow

Superior Dilator 9

Levator of Upper Lip 3

Transverse Dilator of the Nose 10

Lateral Dilator 8

Orbicular
of the Mouth 1

Zygomaticus 4

Depressor of the Lower Lip 5

Ext. Adductor
of the Ear 90

Levator of Upper
Lip and Nostril 2

Levator of Ear 90

Abductor of the Ear 90

Anterior Oblique of the Head 24

Wing of Atlas

Posterior Oblique of the Head 23

Omo-hyoid 15b

Depressor of the Ear 90

Splenius 19
III, IV, V Cerv. Vert.

Facial vein 92 a

Buccinator 6

Masseter 7

Mast. Humeralis 34

Cervical Trapezius 18a

Mastoido-Humeralis 34

Splenius 19

Jugular Vein 92 b

Sterno-Cephalicus 12

Complexus 21

Posterior
Oblique 23

Cervical
Ligament 11

Intertransversales Colli 14
IV-VII Cervical Vertebrae

Shoulder-Blade

Mastoido
Humeralis 34

Rectus Capitis 17

Serratus
Cervicis 39a

Longus Colli 13
I-VII Cervical Vertebrae

Ant. Oblique
of the Head 24

Molars

"Bars" of
the Mouth

Incisor Teeth

Canine Teeth

1

The automatic support of the horse's weight is completed *Automatic* at the fetlock, D, by the Suspensory Ligament (62) and at the *Support* pastern joints, E and F, by the tendons of the Perforans (61) and Perforatus (60) muscles with their check ligaments.

The Suspensory Ligament (62) is a broad elastic cord attached at the back of the knee and cannon bone, very visible towards the lower end of the cannon bone; it divides just above the fetlock into two branches which are inserted on the sesamoid bones, a band passing forward on each side of the joint to the front of the first phalanx, to join the tendon of the Common Digital Extensor (54): see Pl. 6, p. 62.

This arrangement serves two purposes. It supports the fetlock automatically, and by its prolongation to the front prevents the pasterns from knuckling over forwards, much as the tie string below the knee prevents the knee from buckling forward.

To test the principle of the automatic support of the horse by his fore legs, I made a rough model with bits of wood and string like this, and found that a weight, W, representing the downward pull of the body, attached as depicted, was supported by my gimcrack construction. So the muscular effort demanded of the front legs when at rest is apparently no greater than the small muscular adjustments we ourselves make, when standing, to keep the jointed column of our legs upright under our body.

The hind leg, as we noticed in Chapter I, corresponds very closely to the fore leg in the general character and relation of the bones; and the correspondence is close, for it is provided with an inelastic string, the Peronæus Tertius (82), which connects the femur with the cannon bone, much as the Biceps Brachii connects the shoulder blade with the Radius. Yet the hind quarters are not automatically supported

Automatic
Support

without effort on the part of the muscles, since the articulation of the femur with the pelvis falls too far forward in relation to the foot.

Perhaps this is a useful provision for safety, for it keeps the horse 'on his toes', like a good gamesplayer. A horse planted on all four feet would be very slow at getting off the mark.

Action of
Fore Leg

Turn now to the leg's action.[1] At each stride the leg is made by muscular contraction into a rigid spoke, which rotates about a point on the shoulder blade as its axle, and as a rigid spoke it acts until the body has advanced so far that the leg has passed the vertical position. Then, as it can no longer serve as a support, the horse uses it for propulsion

Spoke-like action of the fore legs

by extending the joints. And in this action of the legs the inelastic tissues play a very important part.

Let us follow in more detail the action of the fore leg.

At each stride the leg is put forward with the joints extended, and touches the ground first with the elastic frog at the back of the foot. As the weight settles on to the leg, the pasterns yield elastically, and the Biceps (47) and the Triceps (51), that extended the leg, relax, letting the joints at A and B (Pl. 11, p. 108) close quietly until the body is supported by the inelastic tissues which we have been discussing. When the horse is standing at ease and the pull of his weight is merely directly downwards, the inelastic tissues support him unhelped; but when he is in action, the leg needs to be braced, so the long head of the Triceps muscle (51a) that

[1]See Chap. IX., p. 104.

joins the under edge of the shoulder blade to the point of the *Action of* elbow (Olecranon) contracts, pulling against the inelastic tie *Fore Leg*

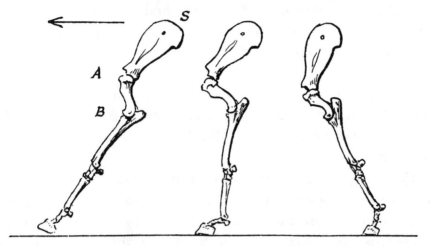

Bones of the left fore leg in action

of the Biceps (47), thus making the triangle ABS absolutely rigid, while, below, the Extensors straighten the knee and

pastern joints. Formed thus into a rigid spoke from shoulder blade to foot, for, as explained, the knee is indirectly braced, the leg is rotated about a point on the upper half of the shoulder blade by the following muscles: the Rhomboid (32), the Serratus Cervicis (39a), the Anterior and Posterior Deep Pectorals (37 and 38), and the Latissimus Dorsi (33). Depicted diagrammatically, the action of these muscles is seen to be tangential (see also Pl. 5, p. 58).

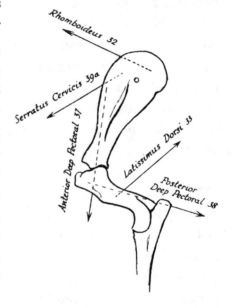

The principle of automatic support is applied also in the carriage of the shoulder. Strands of the Dorso-scapular ligament arising on the withers are inserted on the underside of the shoulder blade; and on its outside the tendinous middle part of the Trapezius (18) is attached to the spine of the shoulder blade. Together they can support the whole fore limb when the foot is off the ground, thus relieving the muscles.

The Dorso-scapular ligaments mingle at their insertion under the shoulder blade with the Serratus Thoracis (39*b*), and the 'pivot point' of the shoulder blade occurs near their junction.

'Point', 'pivot', 'rotate' must not be taken literally; they are figures of speech, useful for discussion and illustration. The 'point' upon the shoulder blade, on which the leg is

*Sliding of
the Shoulder*

pivoted, is not fixed upon the body, for the whole shoulder can slide slightly backwards and forwards. Drawn forward when the foot takes the ground, the shoulder blade has moved back by the end of the stride. Thus the body has not only been advanced by the spoke-like action of the leg and the extension of the leg and shoulder joints, but has crept forward in relation to the shoulder blade during the stride, which results in an additional advance of the body in relation to the foot and the ground over which the horse is travelling.

After the stride, as the spent leg is coming forward, the shoulder blade is drawn forward again along the chest. Thus body and leg alternately creep forward on each other, adding length to the stride, and increasing the horse's speed.[1]

When the body of the horse has advanced so far that the leg has passed the vertical, and the 'pivot point' on the shoulder blade is in front of the foot, the leg is no longer of use for support. Immediately, the joints at A and B are extended by the extensor muscles and the body propelled forwards. To effect this the Long head of the Triceps (51*a*) is relaxed. This frees the shoulder blade, which is then extended on the

[1]See Chap. IX., p. 110.

humerus by the Biceps Brachii muscle (47), and also frees the
elbow joint, which is then extended by the contraction of the
External and Internal heads of the Triceps (51*b* and 51*c*) and
the Anconeus (52). The Long head of the Triceps cannot do
this work, for if used to extend the elbow it would necessarily
pull the shoulder blade back and prevent the desired extension of the shoulder joint by the Biceps; whereas the External

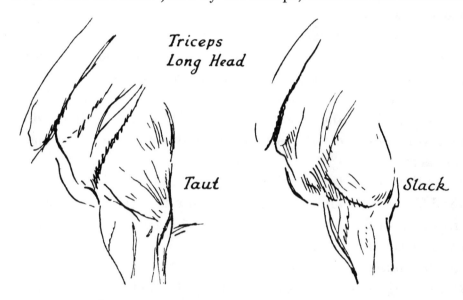

and Internal heads of the Triceps, and the Anconeus, being
attached to the humerus only, extend the elbow joint at
B, without interfering with the freedom of the shoulder
blade.

On the living horse the Long head of the Triceps (51*a*) is
very noticeable as a soft bag-like mass, that hangs over the
elbow joint, when the leg is at rest. When the horse is moving
it tightens and is seen as a firm smooth surface. The working
of this muscle may easily be watched at a quiet walking pace,
and then it will be noticed that the muscle slackens and becomes soft and bag-like again *before* the leg is lifted, as soon,
that is, as it has passed the vertical; which is a confirmation of
the anatomical explanation of its action given above. I had

*Extension of
the Fore Leg*

often observed its moment of relaxation, and was puzzled on the point until I knew the reason.

Such descriptions of muscles and their action are necessarily rather summary. For in the simplest movement innumerable muscles come into play. But once the general principle of the motion of a limb is grasped, the action and effect of many of the less dominant muscles should be sufficiently clear from the plates.

At the end of a stride, when the leg has attained its full extension, the foot is lifted, the knee elbow and shoulder joints are flexed and the leg and shoulder are brought forward together for the next stride, the muscle that does most of this work being the Mastoido-Humeralis (34) which is attached to the humerus and the fascia which cover the shoulder blade and arm.

As the limb advances the shoulder and elbow joints are extended, and the knee and fetlock joints straightened, projecting the foot forwards,[1] ready to take the ground again and to execute the next stride.

*Action of
Hind Leg*

The action of the hind leg resembles that of the fore leg in that it begins by serving as a rigid spoke and ends by the extension of the joints.

As the foot touches the ground the elasticity of the hoof and the play of the pasterns relieve the limb of shock, and muscles such as the Vasti (79) on the top of the femur give way gradually, allowing the weight of the body to settle gently on to the support of the leg.

The bracing of the hind leg is very similar to that of the fore leg. The fore leg, you remember, is locked into a rigid spoke by the contraction of the Triceps, between the shoulder blade and elbow, pulling against the inelastic tissues of the

[1]Marey and Pagés give diagrams of several positions of the legs both in support and suspension in the different paces, plotting the course through which the different joints travel. Many of these diagrams are reproduced in Goubeau and Barrier's *Exterior of the Horse*.

Biceps Brachii (see p. 15). In the hind leg the rigid mass is formed of the femur, tibia and metatarsus, the triangle ABH (Pl. 11, p. 108), by the contraction of the Vasti on the stifle joint, and the Gastrocnemii (80a) between the femur and hock, which pull against the inelastic string of the Peronæus Tertius (82).

Thus locked into a rigid spoke, the hind leg is turned upon the knob of the femur by the action of the Middle Glutæus (68) and the mass of muscles that form the rump.

As soon as the leg is past the point of support, the hip, stifle and hock joints at H, A and B are extended and the horse thrown forward by their thrust. Most of the muscles on the quarters help in this extension (see Pls. 8 and 9). On the front of the leg the Rectus Femoris (79a), the External and Internal Vasti (79b, 79c) extend the femur on the tibia —not the tibia on the femur, because the foot is the fixed point from which all the bones get their resistance for propelling the body. They are powerful muscles which correspond to the strong muscles on the top of your own thigh. Behind the leg, the muscles which form the rump help to extend this and the other joints by pulling the leg back with tremendous power: the Biceps Femoris (70), the Semimembranosus (72), the Semitendinosus (71), the Adductor (76), and the Glutæus muscles (68 and 69). How great the mass of these muscles is may be seen by looking at a horse from behind, as well as from the side.[1] The sketch overleaf is from a 'Trait du Nord' draught horse, a crossbred French and Belgian stallion.

Simultaneously with the extension of hip and stifle joints, the hock joint is extended by the Gastrocnemii (80a), which pull on the Tendo Achillis (80b). But the Gastrocnemii, the calf muscles, which are relatively much less developed than in man, are not strong enough to do the work of extending the hock by themselves, or to take up the strain often thrown

[1]See Chap. IX., p. 110.

Action of
Hind Leg

upon them, and so they are helped by an ingenious contrivance of parallel tendons, the Peronæus Tertius (82) and the Superficial Digital Flexor (86), which compel the power applied to the one joint to act upon the other.

In Pl. 11 (p. 108) these tendons are represented diagrammatically. They join the hock to the femur on the upper side of the tibia, and the cannon bone (Metatarsus) to the femur on its under side. Being inextensible and working in parallel they compel these two joints, stifle and hock, A and B, to open and

close together, and the muscular force of the quarters, exerted directly on the stifle, is indirectly exerted equally on the hock. Thus the powerful extension of the stifle by the Vasti muscles extends the hock through the pull of the femur on the Tendo *Action of* Achillis (80*b*), and the extension of the hock by the contrac- *Hind Leg* tion of the Gastrocnemii (80*a*) contributes to the extension of the stifle by the pull of the tibia on the Peronæus Tertius (82). It is this simultaneous extension of both joints that makes the action of the quarters so effective.[1]

Below the knee and hock the legs are practically only bones *Fetlock and* and strings. *Pasterns*

On the front of the legs the mechanism is very simple, the tendons of the Common (54, 84) and Lateral (55, 85) Extensors pulling the pasterns forwards into the position in which the foot is at the right inclination to take the ground.

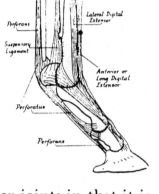

At the back of the legs the mechanism is more intricate and more interesting, with the three strings which support the weight of the body and help in its propulsion. They are the Suspensory Ligament (62, 89) and the Perforatus (60, 86) and Perforans (61, 87) tendons.

The fetlock joint differs from the other joints in that it is *Over-* 'overextended' when supporting the weight of the horse, the *extension* pasterns inclining forwards in front of the line of the cannon bone. And the more important duties of the Perforatus and Perforans tendons are to support the fetlock joint and pasterns, and to straighten them in the act of galloping and jumping. Their true flexing action of lifting the foot occurs only when the foot is off the ground.

Generally speaking, the Suspensory Ligament, Perforatus *Back* and Perforans support the first, second and third phalanges, *Tendons* respectively.

Let us first consider the action of the tendons as supports to the fetlock and pasterns.

[1]See Chap. IX., p. 111.

Plate 2. Lower Layer of the Muscles of the Body

[The numbers printed after the names of muscles are the numbers of the other plates in which the muscles appear.
The plates in which the muscles are best shown are numbered in heavier type.]

*Numbers
and Colours
of the Muscles*

11.	Buff	*Cervical Ligament.* Pl. 1.
12.	Yellow	*Sterno-Cephalicus.* Pl. 1, 3, 10.
15b.	Mauve	*Omo-hyoideus.* Pl. 1, 2, 3, 10.
17.	Yellow	*Rectus Capitis.* Pl. 1.
20.	Blue	*Longissimus Capitis.*
20.	Yellow	*Longissimus Atlantis.*
21.	Red	*Complexus.* Pl. 1.
22.	Red	*Multifidus Cervicis.*
23.	Mauve	*Posterior Oblique of the head.* Pl. 1.
25a.	Mauve	*Serratus Posterior.* Pl. 3.
25b.	Red	*External Intercostals.* Pl. 3.
26.	Yellow	*Transversalis Costarum.*
27.	Red	*Longissimus Dorsi.* Pl. 8.
27a.	Red	*Spinalis Dorsi.*
50a.	Green	*External Oblique of the Abdomen.* Pl. 3, 7, 8, 9, 10. It is cut to show the Internal Oblique, 30b.
30b.	Blue	*Internal Oblique of the Abdomen.* Pl. 8.
32.	Green	*Rhomboideus.* Pl. 3, 4, 5.
35.	Yellow	*Anterior Superficial Pectoral.* Pl. 3, 5, 10.
37.	Green	*Anterior Deep Pectoral.* Pl. 4, 5, 10.
38.	Red	*Posterior Deep Pectoral.* Pl. 3, 4, 5, 10.
39a.	Mauve	*Serratus Cervicis.* Pl. 1, 3, 4, 5.
39b.	Mauve	*Serratus Thoracis.* Pl. 3, 4, 5, 11.
41.	Blue	*Supraspinatus.* Pl. 4.
42.	Red	*Infraspinatus.* Pl. 4.

*Numbers
and Colours
of the Muscles*

43.	Green	*Teres Minor.* Pl. 4.
47.	Green	*Biceps Brachii.* Pl. 4, 6, 10, 11.
49.	Blue	*Brachialis Anticus.* Pl. 3, 4, 6, 10.
51a. 51b.	Yellow	*Triceps Brachii.* Pl. 3, 4, 6.
53.	Mauve	*External Radial Extensor (Extensor Carpi Radialis).* Pl. 3, 4, 6, 10, 11.
54.	Green	*Common Digital Extensor.* Pl. 3, 4, 6, 10, 11.
55.	Yellow	*Lateral Digital Extensor.* Pl. 3, 4, 6, 10.
59.	Blue	*External Flexor of the Metacarpus (Extensor carpi Ulnaris).* Pl. 3, 4, 6, 10.
64b.	Yellow	*Iliacus.* Pl. 7, 8.
68a.	Mauve	*Middle Gluteus (Gl. Medius).* Pl. 7, 8, 11.
71.	Green	*Semitendinosus.* Pl. 3, 7, 8, 9, 11.
72.	Blue	*Semimembranosus.* Pl. 2, 7, 8, 9, 11.
79a.	Red	*Rectus Femoris.* Pl. 3, 7, 8, 9, 11.
79b.	Yellow	*External Vastus.* Pl. 3, 7, 8, 9, 11.
80a.	Blue	*Gastrocnemius.* Pl. 3, 7, 8, 9, 11.
81.	Red	*Soleus.* Pl. 3, 7, 9, 11.
84.	Green	*Anterior or Long Digital Extensor.* Pl. 3, 7, 9, 11.
85.	Yellow	*Lateral Digital Extensor.* Pl. 3, 7, 9.
87.	Mauve	*Deep Digital Flexor (Perforans).* Pl. 3, 7, 9, 11.
92b.	Blue	*Jugular Vein.* Pl. 1, 3, 10.
92d.	Blue	*External Thoracic Vein.* Pl. 3.

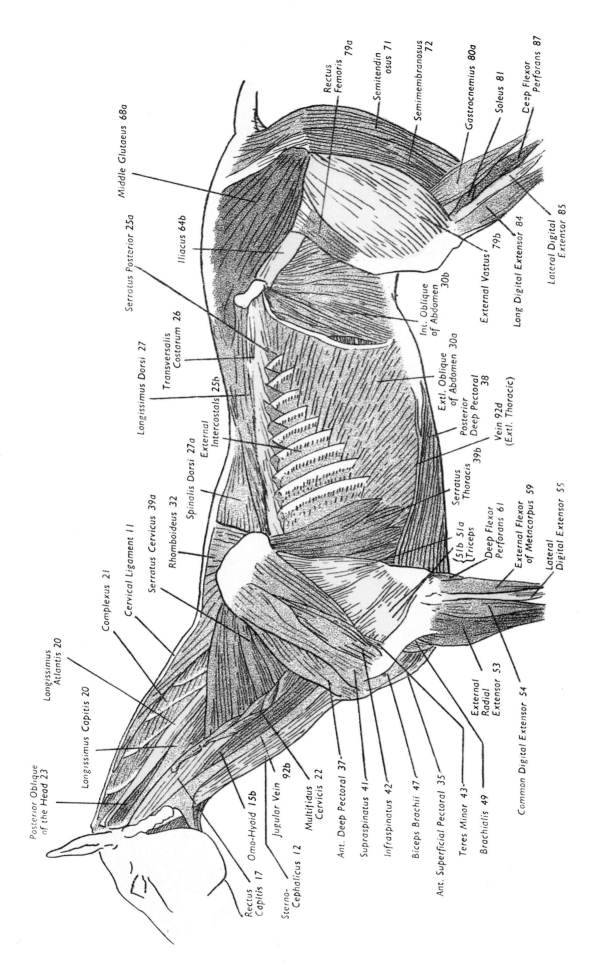

2

Rectus Femoris 79a

Semitendin osus 71

Semimembranosus 72

Gastrocnemius 80a

Soleus 81

Deep Flexor Perforans 87

Middle Glutaeus 68a

Serratus Posterior 25a

Iliacus 64b

Int. Oblique of Abdomen 30b

External Vastus 79b

Long Digital Extensor 84

Lateral Digital Extensor 85

Longissimus Dorsi 27

Transversalis Costarum 26

Longissimus Dorsi 25b

External Intercostals 25h

Spinalis Dorsi 27a

Extl. Oblique of Abdomen 30a

Posterior Deep Pectoral 38

Vein 92d (Extl. Thoracic)

Serratus Thoracis 39b

Rhomboideus 32

Serratus Cervicus 39a

Cervical Ligament 11

Complexus 21

{51b 51a (Triceps}

Deep Flexor Perforans 61

External Flexor of Metacarpus 59

Lateral Digital Extensor 55

Longissimus Atlantis 20

Longissimus Capitis 20

Posterior Oblique of the Head 23

Rectus Capitis 17

Sterno-Cephalicus 12

Omo-Hyoid 15b

Jugular Vein 92b

Multifidus Cervicis 22

Ant. Deep Pectoral 37

Supraspinatus 41

Infraspinatus 42

Biceps Brachii 47

Ant. Superficial Pectoral 35

Teres Minor 43

Brachialis 49

External Radial Extensor 53

Lateral Digital Extensor 54

Common Digital Extensor 54

The Suspensory Ligament running down the back of the cannon bone is divided into two branches which are inserted on the sesamoid bones, and, as the sesamoid bones are attached by ligaments to the second and chiefly the first phalanx, the Suspensory Ligament is in effect attached to the pasterns; the sesamoids, which might be called the Patellæ of the fetlock joint, helping it to slip backwards and forwards over the joint.

The Suspensory Ligament is an elastic cord, purely automatic in action. It serves as a spring, helping to support the fetlock joint; its chief duty is apparently to eliminate abruptness and shock in the action of the fetlock and pasterns.

The Perforatus and Perforans tendons, being controlled by muscles, are not automatic in action, like the Suspensory Ligament, until they reach their limit of extension, when their check strings support them instead of the muscles.

The check string of the Perforatus is strong in both fore and hind leg; that of the Perforans is weak and sometimes even non-existent in the hind leg.

Thus the horse has for his support all the three strings which are at the back of the leg.

Now let us study their action as propulsive agents.

The Suspensory Ligament helps, for its automatic elasticity is always attempting to pull the pasterns back. If in the leg of a dead horse the Perforatus and Perforans tendons are cut and the pasterns overextended, pulled well forward, and let go, the Suspensory Ligament will pull them back into line with the cannon bone, but no farther.

The Superficial Flexor (the Perforatus) differs notably in the fore and hind legs, for muscular as it is in the fore leg, it is hardly more than a tendon in the hind leg; even in the fore leg it is very weak in comparison with the Deep Digital Flexor (the Perforans).

It was stated previously that these tendons were limited in their movement by check strings; to be accurate, in the hind leg the Perforatus tendon is attached directly to the hock. The attachment, however, allows the tendon, which forms a sort of cap over the tuber calcis, to slip to and fro. When the pasterns give under pressure, it slips down to its limit, and the fetlock is then automatically supported from its attachment on the hock. When the hock is flexed, the Perforatus tendon is tightened by the movement of the tuber calcis, and the foot, if off the ground, is bent backwards. But the pull is not very strong, for the foot can always be overextended, in whatever position the limb is, as may be tested on the leg of a dead horse and seen in instantaneous photographs.

The Perforatus, indeed, exerts very little propulsive power in comparison with the Perforans.

The Perforans is the principal agent in the action of the pasterns. A very powerful muscle in both fore and hind legs, it pulls the pasterns back from the overextended position with such energy that it lifts the fetlock and leg with great effect.

Its action is very effective in adding to length of stride and leap, because it takes place when the body is already on the move from the extension of other joints. Everyone must have noticed in gymnastics how effective a very slight push is in helping someone who is vaulting to clear the vaulting horse. In all muscular movement little contributions of force add enormously to the resulting action. When a horse raises his forehand into the air, he does not only extend his shoulder, elbow, and fetlock joints, but adds to this the contraction of the big Serratus muscle, which lifts his body in relation to the shoulder blade, which is itself rising through the action of the joints.

Distant transmission of power makes for activity. It makes large calf muscles unnecessary, and avoids the putting of weight low down on the leg, which is destructive of agility. Deer and hare also have these parallel strings, but not dogs or cats. In deer, which jump so wonderfully, the legs are noticeably light, mere bones with strings to work the joints. Light extremities are indispensable to speed, for in any movement the foot, being stationary on the ground, is sheer dead weight to be lifted by the impetus acquired by the body. Indeed all the sections of the leg, since they are advancing less rapidly than the body which they propel, are in varying degrees a check to its advance. Put simply, do you put on heavy boots when you jump?

The Back Tendons

When a horse is lying down the action of the strings is very clearly shown by the way in which his leg is tightly bent at the stifle, hock and fetlock (see Tailpiece to the Preface).

We noticed, in studying the fore legs, how the sliding of the shoulder blade and body reciprocally on each other added to the length of the stride. In the hind leg there is, of course, no sliding movement, since the head of the femur is socketed into the pelvis. There is, however, a slight swing of the pelvis and sacrum which gives a similar result. Forward at the moment the foot takes the ground, it swings backward while the leg is in action, thus lengthening the stride; and when the leg is raised and is coming forward again, it is pulled forward again for the next stride. A sprinter uses this principle, swinging his hips as he runs.

Swing of the Pelvis

Later I will refer to the economical way in which such movements are effected.

You will see, when a horse's leg is fully extended, a taut line running downwards from the big knob on the pelvis to the stifle. It is the Tensor Fasciæ Latæ (66) acting as a check to prevent him from over-stretching the joints of the leg.

Reference has already been made to fetlock joint and pasterns, but they are such important parts of the mechanism of a horse's leg that it is worth while studying them more fully. By their elasticity they not only serve to reduce shock, but

Fetlock and Pasterns

Fetlock and Pasterns   also add to the smoothness of the action in general. Extended in a straight line with the leg when the foot takes the ground, they give way, they 'overextend', as the weight of the body comes on to them, and recover themselves after the leg has passed the vertical position. By shortening and lengthening in this way, they keep the horse's body nearly at the same level throughout the stride. If you will put a crutch or broom handle under your armpit you will realize very clearly the advantage of their mechanism. When the foot of the crutch is put on the ground in front of you its top is lowered, rising as you advance, till it reaches the vertical position, when it lifts your armpit very awkwardly, dropping again as you leave it behind you. By the play of the pastern, this rising and falling motion is avoided in the horse's leg, and its body travels nearly on a level, the action gaining in speed and economy of effort. You may see a thoroughbred's supple pastern bent at right angles to the leg, parallel with the ground,[1] the ergot at times even actually touching it.

The Foot   Another interesting detail of the action is the sudden way in which the foot is lifted at the end of the stride, so characteristic of a thoroughbred, that there may be no risk of its striking an irregularity of the ground, as the leg is swung forward. The work is not left to the Perforans muscle (61), as muscular contraction might not be rapid enough, but is performed by the elasticity of the tendons and the Inferior Sesamoid ligaments, which, being stretched when the foot is down, flick the foot up instantaneously, as soon as it is free of the ground.

This principle of the flick is used again in the astragalus, the 'wheel' of the hock joint, which is not quite regular in its movement, so that when the joint is in action the pull of the muscles is pent up for a moment and is released with a sudden flip, like the movement of the blade of a penknife, that adds acceleration to the thrust of the leg.

[1]See Chap. IX, p. 112.

Before leaving the legs let me refer to another arrangement. It is important that the foot of the lifted leg, when
being brought forward, should not collide with the other leg
that is upon the ground.

In the fore leg this clearance is effected by the movement of
the shoulder blade rather than that of the leg. In a well-made
horse the foreleg should bend almost straight at the knee, for
if the foot throws outwards exaggeratedly, this 'dishing' results in waste of energy
and loss of speed. Owing
to the chest being shaped
like the prow of a boat,
the shoulder blade as it
slips forward turns its
front edge inwards, which
throws the elbow and foot
outwards so that the foot
advances quite clear of the
other leg. Another con-
sequence of this move-
ment of the shoulder
blade is that when the leg is
extended the foot is brought
under the middle line of
the body, which makes
for speed and easy action.

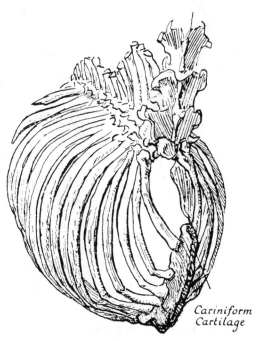

Cariniform
Cartilage

Bony thorax of the horse: front view

In the hind leg this clearance is effected by the shape of the
hock joint, in which the 'wheel' of the joint (the astragalus) is
set slightly outwards, so that the foot is carried outwards
as it comes forward. This outward turn of the astragalus is
necessary to compensate the movement of the femur; for the
end of the femur is thrown outwards in coming forward, that
the stifle may clear the flank—a free outward action is said by
some authorities to be essential to speed. As a result of the

Clearance of the Foot outward throw of the femur, the tibia and hock are inclined towards the middle line of the body, which might cause the foot, as the leg advances, to strike the other leg which is on the ground, if it was not itself swung outwards from the hock by the setting of the astragalus.

In fore leg and hind leg alike the foot, when it is being extended to begin the stride, is brought on to or near to the middle line of the body: particularly so in a thoroughbred, for this prevents yawing of the body, making for speed and economy of effort in progression. In a very fast gallop the footmarks may lie in a true line 'as if made by the spokes of a wheel without a felloe'.

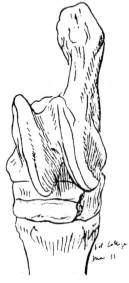

Spiral Progression

Left Hock, front view. Cf. inside view on p. 44.

Animal progression is spiral. There is the forward movement, the rise and fall, and the lateral oscillation of the body, as it is supported alternately by the right and left legs. For rapid progression the rising and falling motion and the lateral yawing should be reduced to the least possible minimum as it is in a racehorse. The rising and falling motion is reduced by the play of the pasterns and other elasticities; and the sideways oscillation by bringing the feet as nearly as possible under the centre line of the body. Ducks walk so notoriously badly because their legs are short and set on so far apart that they cannot put their feet well under their bodies, and so must waddle their bodies right and left over their feet.

The Vertebral Column   Let us leave the legs and turn to the backbone.

It is knitted together with innumerable muscles both underneath and on the upper side, the latter of which in a well-fed horse build up the shape of the back. The movement of these muscles is not perceptible in themselves, though occasionally strings show momentarily on the loins.

The ribs are connected by sheets of muscles which consolidate the body. Though they do not show as individual muscles the effect of their action is very noticeable in the changes they cause in the position and visibility of the ribs.

The vertebræ of the neck, like those of the back, are interconnected by an intricate web of muscles (see Pl. 1), which make of the cervical column a sort of stiffish hawser, as can be seen in the living animal when the neck is strongly bent. The section of the neck is in general oval, narrower on the top and thicker towards the underside, with the strong Mastoido-Humeral (34) muscles which attach it to the trunk.

The shape of the back is built up by the Longissimus Dorsi (27), the longest muscle of the body, which, running from the hips to the neck, fills the angle between the upright processes of the spine and the sideway processes of the loins and tops of the ribs. When in a gallop the spine is flexed to bring the hind legs well forward at the beginning of a stride, the Longissimus Dorsi, by its powerful extension of the spine, adds to the propulsion of the hind limb.

When looking at the skeleton we noticed that the shape of the withers is made by the enormous bony processes that support the neck and head. From them there run to the neck not only muscles, but the Cervical Ligament (11): see Pl. 1, p. 12. Formed of elastic tissue, and divided into strands, which run to the different cervical vertebræ and to the base of the skull, it undertakes the work of supporting the head and neck. In the giraffe it is enormously developed, as may be expected, and takes its purchase the whole way down the creature's spine!

Plate 3. Upper Layer of the Muscles of the Body

[*The numbers printed after the names of muscles are the numbers of the other plates in which the muscles appear. The plates in which the muscles are best shown are numbered in heavier type.*]

*Numbers
and Colours
of the Muscles*

12. Yellow Sterno-Cephalicus. Pl. 1, 2, 10.
15b. Mauve Omo-hyoideus. Pl. 2, 10.
16a. Green Cutaneous muscle of the neck. Pl. 3, 10.
18a. Blue Trapezius, Cervical part. Pl. 1, 4, 5.
18b. Blue Trapezius, Dorsal part. Pl. 4, 5.
19. Yellow Splenius. Pl. 1, 10.
25a. Mauve Serratus posterior. Pl. 2.
25b. Red External Intercostals. Pl. 2.
29. Buff Abdominal Tunic.
30a. Green External Oblique of the abdomen.
     Pl. 2, 7, 8, 10.
32. Green Rhomboideus. Pl. 2, 4, 5.
33. Green Latissimus Dorsi. Pl. 4, 5, 10.
34. Red Mastoido-Humeralis. Pl. 1, 4, 5, 10.
35. Yellow Anterior Superficial Pectoral. Pl. 2,
     5, 10.
38. Red Posterior Deep Pectoral. Pl. 2, 4, 5, 10.
39a. Mauve Serratus Cervicis. Pl. 1, 2, 4, 5.
39b. Mauve Serratus Thoracis. Pl. 2, 4, 5, 11.
40. Mauve Deltoid. Pl. 4.
49. Blue Brachialis Anticus. Pl. 2, 4, 6, 10.
51. Yellow Triceps Brachii. Pl. 2, 4, 6.
53. Mauve External Radial Extensor (*Extr. Carpi
     Radialis*). Pl. 2, 4, 6, 10, 11.

*Numbers
and Colours
of the Muscles*

54. Green Common Digital Extensor (*Extensor
     pedis*). Pl. 2, 4, 6, 10, 11.
55. Yellow Lateral Digital Extensor (*Extr. Digiti
     Quinti*). Pl. 2, 4, 6, 10.
59. Blue External Flexor of the Metacarpus
     (*Ulnaris Lateralis*). Pl. 2, 4, 6, 10.
66. Mauve Tensor fasciæ latæ. Pl. 7, 8, 11.
67. Blue Superficial Gluteus. Pl. 7, 8.
70. Red Biceps femoris. Pl. 7, 8, 9, 11.
71. Green Semitendinosus. Pl. 2, 7, 8, 9, 11.
79a. Red Rectus femoris. Pl. 2, 7, 8, 9, 11.
79b. Yellow External Vastus (*V. Lateralis*). Pl. 2,
     7, 8, 9, 11.
80a. Blue Gastrocnemius. Pl. 2, 7, 8, 9, 11.
81. Red Soleus. Pl. 2, 7, 9, 11.
84. Green Anterior or Long Digital Extensor
     (*Extr. pedis*). Pl. 2, 7, 9, 11.
85. Yellow Lateral Digital Extensor. Pl. 2, 7, 9.
87. Mauve Deep Digital Flexor (*Perforans*).
     Pl. 2, 7, 9, 11.
92b. Blue Jugular Vein. Pl. 1, 2, 10.
92d. Blue. External Thoracic Vein. Pl. 2.

Semitendinosus 71

Biceps Femoris 70

Gastrocnemius 80a

Soleus 81

Deep Flexor Perforans 87

Superficial Glutaeus 67

Fascia

Tensor Fasciae Latae 66

Serratus Posterior 25a

Lateral Digl. Extr. 85

Ant. Digl. Extensor 84

External Vastus 79b

Rectus Femoris 79a

Fascia of the Thigh

Ext. Oblique of Abdomen 30a

Abdominal Tunic 29

External -Intercostals 25b

Latissimus Dorsi 33

Triceps Brachii 51

Deltoid 40

Serratus Thoracis 39b

Vein 92d

Posterior Deep Pectoral 38

External Flexor 59

Lateral Digital Extr. 55

Deep Flx. Perforans 61

Trapezius Dorsal, 18b

Trapezius Cervical 18a

Serratus Cervicis 39a

Rhomboideus 32

Splenius 19

Omo-Hyoideus 15b

Jugular Vein 92

Sterno-Cephalicus 12

Cutaneous Muscle 16a

Mastoido-Humeralis 34

Ant. Superficial Pectoral 35

Brachialis 49

External Radial Extr. 53

Common Digital Extensor 54

Without such automatic support a horse could hardly keep *Cervical* its head up. Muscles, which suffice for occasionally tossing and *Ligament* raising the head and neck, would quickly become exhausted if asked to support them uninterruptedly. Everyone knows in his own person how quickly the human neck gets tired, short as it is, when it is held in a horizontal position.

It is very noticeable how a tired horse, especially one draw- *Swing of the* ing a load, swings its head from side to side. The reason for *Head* the movement is, I think, as follows.

There runs along each side of the neck a long broad muscle, the Mastoido-Humeral (34), which is attached to the shoulder

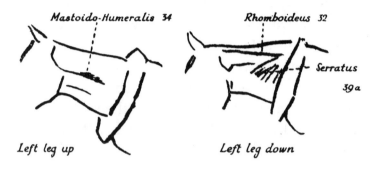

blade and humerus at one end and to the mastoid pro-cess of the head and the top of the neck at the other (see Pl. 3). When a horse is walking, this muscle draws forward the shoulder blade and leg that is lifted from the ground. To do this it pulls upon the head, which tends to bend the neck to the side. Simultaneously, as the fore leg on the other side of the horse is in action, the Rhomboideus (32) and Cervical part of the Serratus (39a), attached to the shoulder blade, are pull-ing the neck in the opposite direction. Working thus on op-posite sides of the neck they counterbalance one another. The Serratus certainly is pulling much more energetically than the Mastoido-Humeralis, but, as its five strands are inserted to the lower cervical vertebræ, it is pulling at the base of the neck, while the Mastoido-Humeralis, through its attachment to the

Swing of the Head

skull, is pulling at its extremity. The gain in leverage through this longer purchase compensates the latter for its weaker action and allows its influence on the neck to counterbalance that of its opponent.

It must not be supposed that these are the only muscles involved. Muscular action is so intricate that the larger movements alone can be discussed. The Splenius (19), the Longissimus Capitis and Atlantis (20) and other muscles that extend and bend the neck join in as required.

This balancing of muscular action in the neck occurs apparently only when a horse is fresh; when he is tired he swings his head sideways at each stride to spare his muscles. It is in principle what we do on a bicycle when we are tired. We throw our weight sideways at each stroke that the impetus of the body may give a thrust to the pedal and reduce the demand upon the muscles. The horse, by flinging his neck and head away from the shoulder that is working, similarly saves himself effort. If you will watch a horse closely you will see that this fling is exactly timed to the effort of the leg.

Movement of the Pelvis

This mutual help of the shoulder blades is an instance of the economy of effort which occurs in the action of muscles all over the body.

In the pelvis there is a similar mutual action between the right and left sides. When the right leg, for instance, is at work on the ground and the left leg is lifted, we see the left half of the pelvis swing forward. This action, which adds to the forward reach of the stride, and is taken by the left leg for its own needs, helps the action of the other leg. By pulling forward the left side of the pelvis, it swings the right side of it backwards; or, to put it more accurately, the true turning point of the movement of the pelvis is the head of the right femur, which is supported through the thrust of the leg and foot against the ground, and the pelvis, turning upon it as its fulcrum, advances its point of attachment to the backbone, that is, the body in general.

The swinging movement takes place in the lumbar vertebræ. The pelvis is swung forward by the Longissimus Dorsi (27) and other muscles; the Longissimus Dorsi also steadying the vertebræ of the back, and preventing wrenching in the coupling of the pelvis with the lumbar vertebræ. The swing of the pelvis is similar to the action of rowing. The water, which is the fulcrum to the blade of the oar, corresponds to the head of the femur; the rowlock, the resistance point on the boat, corresponds to the point of attachment of the pelvis to the backbone; and the pull of the oarsman corresponds to the pull of the muscles that advance the left side of the pelvis, which is the handle of the oar.

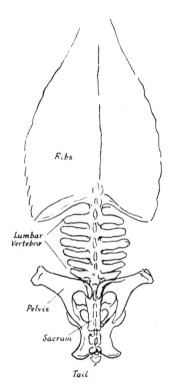

Another instance of the reciprocal help of the parts of the body is seen in this action. The Internal and External Oblique muscles of the Abdomen (30a, 30b), which help to pull the point of the pelvis forward when the leg is up, support the body from the pelvis when the leg is on the ground. Contracting for the former purpose they are taut, and so ready to take up the weight of the body as the stride begins. The contraction and relaxation of these muscles at each stride is very noticeable.

The more one studies the muscles, the more one sees not only how they help each other, but how the muscles and movements involved in one act prepare for the next act. And

Reciprocal the more one watches their action for enjoyment's sake, the
Action of more one becomes aware of the design that results from the
Muscles interplay and contrast of slack and taut and from 'the variety
which is produced by the alternate action and repose of the
muscles'.

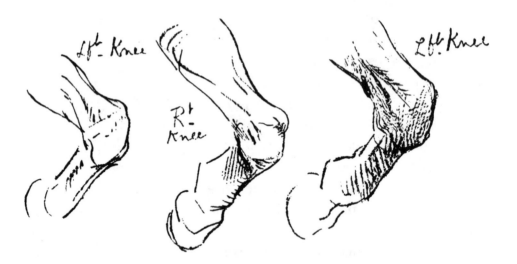

Right and left knees drawn from raised fore legs: see p. 49.

Chapter III. The Skeleton

The bones are very important because they explain the muscles. Even where their forms do not directly affect the surface, their influence is felt in the lie and shape of the muscles.

Diagrams in a book can give no real idea of their shapes in the round. That can only be seen in the skeleton. At the Natural History Museum at South Kensington there are several skeletons of horses on view.

Draw some bones or, better still, model them; their forms are very interesting. It will explain the purpose of their twists and channels, and the structural thrust and pull of one part of the skeleton against another will become clear to you, as the strains in a building are to an architect, so that what he sees is not dead stone but a living organism.

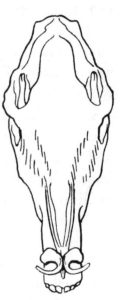

The Skull

In the living horse the surface forms of the head follow the shapes of the bones of the skull very closely. It is only under the nose and lips, and the large Masseter muscle of the jaw, that its shapes are entirely hidden. The Supraorbital ridge over the eye, the Zygomatic ridge on the cheek to which the Masseter muscle is attached, and the shape of the profile are very important landmarks in the construction of the skull; and a thing it

Skull, with Alar Cartilages

is useful to notice is the position of the orifice of the ear, for it is very difficult to place the ear correctly in drawing a horse, owing to its mobility.

35

The Nostrils The shape of the nostrils is made partly by the hooks of cartilage on which they are supported. The tip of one of these

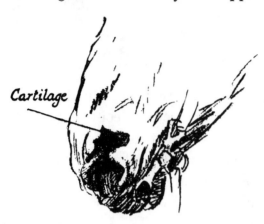

Cartilage

hooks is seen in the attached sketch of a horse whose nose was torn in a fight. The cartilages are so attached that they move very freely.

The absence of teeth in a section of the jaw called the 'Bars' is very convenient for bridling a horse, the more so that it occurs opposite the corner of the mouth. This gap also affects the expression of the face.

The Jaw The 'hinge', the condyle, of the jawbone has a very long bearing sideways, allowing a lateral movement of the jaw in mastication. This sideways movement is often noticeable when a horse yawns.

From the underside the bones of the lower jaw and the deep cleft between them are seen very distinctly. The lower jaw bones are surprisingly narrow, the molars only just overlapping the inner edges of the molars in the upper jaw, which facilitates the sideways grinding movement.

When a horse is eating, the coronoid process of the lower jaw can be seen moving in the hollow just above the eye.

The Neck The two top bones of the neck, the atlas and axis, differ markedly in conformation from the other five (see Pl. 1, p. 12, and p. 7, Chap. I). The balanced mobility of the head results from the movements of these two bones in combination; the skull being hung from the atlas bone, on which it has only an up-and-down movement, the atlas bone being pivoted on the axis bone, on which it can only rotate. The allotment of these two movements to different bones gives mobility without loss of strength, which would result if one bone had to undertake both movements. *The Neck*

The other five bones of the neck, being connected by ball and socket joints, have a movement on each other which is

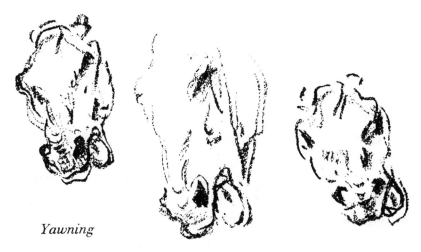

Yawning

free in all directions; but this freedom is limited in scope from mechanical necessity; else the neck, which may be described as a limb with eight articulations, would be wobbly like a chain, and unable to carry the head securely, or support the pull of the muscles which operate the shoulder blade and leg.

When a horse is trying to reach far back, perhaps to mouth his hind foot, his neck forms a strained curve, only free at its extremities. The freest articulation is that of the seventh cervical vertebra with the first vertebra of the thorax, which permits the easy lowering of the neck as in grazing.

Of the bones of the neck the only part that is visible in the living animal is the ridge of the atlas bone just behind the head. So prominent is it that the hollow below it when the head is sharply turned makes a pocket of shadow. *Prominence of Atlas Bone*

The ribs and backbone form the 'chassis' of the horse, to use a motor manufacturer's term, and they resemble it in firmness and elasticity. A chassis must be not only strong but *The Ribs and Backbone*

The Ribs and Backbone   capable of supporting much torsion, if it is to stand up to its work.

The form of the horse's thorax and ribs, its 'barrel', is worth studying, as the shape of the horse's exterior follows them very closely, and the movements of the shoulder blade are affected by the form of the chest, which is very like the prow of a boat (see p. 27).

The Withers   The processes which form the withers rise so high in a horse that its shoulder blades never show above the line of the back, as they do in a dog and still more in a cat. But horses are comparatively stiff and incapable of crouching (see Frontispiece).

The Pelvis   The points of the pelvis show very distinctly in the live horse, and still more noticeably in a cow: the haunch (the ilium), which is the most noticeable, and the buttock (the ischium). From our point of view the pelvic girdle and the sacrum may be considered to be a solid mass, from which many powerful muscles arise.

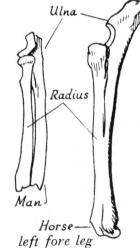

Ulna

Radius

Man

Horse—
left fore leg

The Legs   In bone construction a horse's legs are simpler than are the limbs of man and many other animals with their several fingers and toes. They are formed of what is practically a series of single bones. And the simplification of the bones simplifies the muscular mechanism.

The Forearm   The Ulna and Radius, separate bones in the human arm, are welded into one in the horse, the ulna being reduced merely to the elbow (the olecranon). Hence the horse has no power of rotating his arm, which simplifies the muscular construction below the elbow joint.

The Tibia   In the hind leg, instead of two complete bones below the stifle, such as we have below the knee, the horse has

a strongly developed tibia with a very rudimentary fibula *The Tibia*
attached.

In fore and hind legs alike, the cannon bones, which corre- *The Cannon*
spond to the bones of the back of our hand and instep, are *Bones*
single bones with two rudimen-
tary bones, the splint bones,
attached to the back of them.
Columns of support, they are
dense, hard, strong and almost
cylindrical, those of the fore leg
being the stronger. The splint
bones are rudimentary second
and fourth fingers.

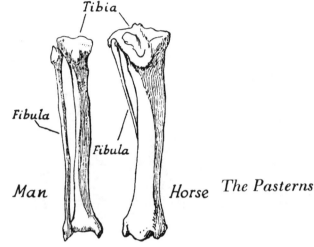

Right Leg : Front view

The cannon bones are sup-
ported at the fetlock joint upon
the three phalanges of the pas- *The Pasterns*
tern, which correspond to our
finger bones, to be exact to the
bones of our third finger. As the
fore leg carries more weight than the hind leg, its pastern
bones are shorter and thicker.

Finally, we reach the hoof, another apparatus designed to *The Hoof*
reduce shock, with its construction of horny conical shell and
elastic pads and cushions.

At many places on the living horse the bones of the leg *Visible Bone*
approach the surface. The spine of the shoulder blade can be *Forms*
detected, and often the outline of the shoulder blade at the
top.

At the 'point of the shoulder' (the scapulo-humeral articulation) the tuberosity of the humerus is very noticeable, as is
the elbow (the olecranon) at the next articulation. On the
inside of the forearm between the flexor and extensor muscles, the bone lies close under the skin, showing very sharply
on the inside of the knee; indeed the bones of the actual knee,

Plate 4. Bones and Muscles of the Shoulder Blade and Arm

[*The numbers printed after the names of muscles are the numbers of the other plates in which the muscles appear. The plates in which the muscles are best shown are numbered in heavier type.*]

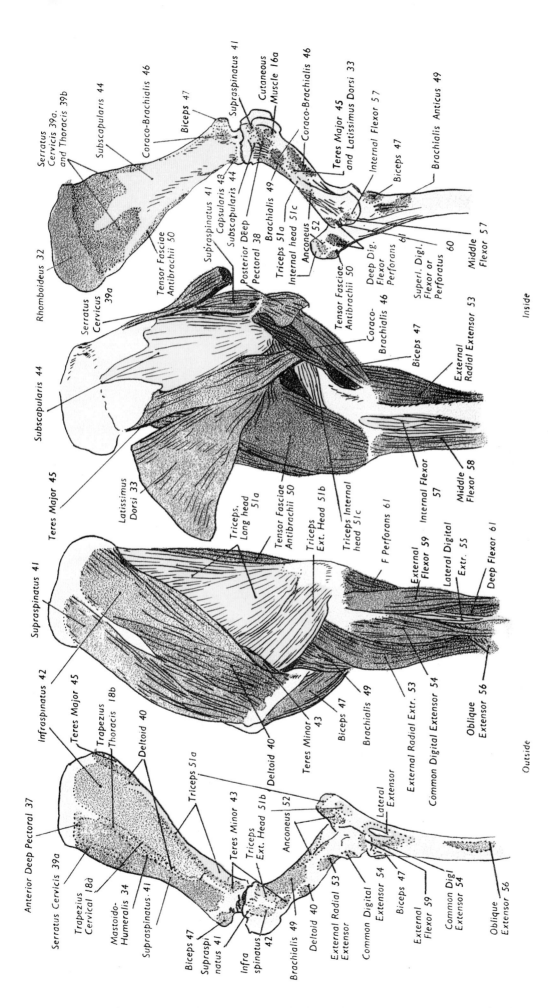

the carpal bones, can almost be counted on a thin-skinned horse. Below the knee the leg is only bone and tendons.

On the hind leg, the point that next after the haunch attracts attention is the trochanter of the femur, which can be seen working under the flesh.

At the stifle the form of the big head of the femur with the knee-cap is very distinct, also the top of the tibia, especially on the inside of the leg.

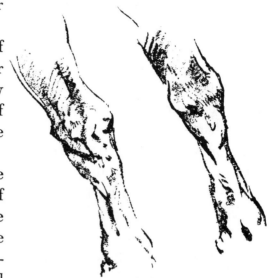

On the inside of the tibia, as on the inside of the radius, where the muscles do not cover the bone, its shape and hardness are very evident; until at the hock and thence to the foot the leg is only bone and tendons. The two sketches of the inside of the right hind leg illustrate how the bone forms show in action.

As our eye runs down the legs three small bones on each catch our attention; on the fore leg the pisiform bone behind the knee and the two sesamoid bones at the fetlock; on the hind leg the knee-cap (the patella) on the front of the stifle, and the two sesamoids. They all help the work of the tendons by giving them more leverage through deflecting, like pulleys, the direction of their pull from its parallelism with the line of the leg.

Articulations or joints are terms which include all unions of bones or cartilages, mobile or rigid, but for our purpose we need only study those that noticeably move.

The motor efficiency of the skeleton depends upon the combination of rigidity and elasticity, for even the hardest

Articulations bones need to be protected against shock. It is not uncommon for a racehorse when galloping to split a pastern bone if his foot hits a stone. Thus the skeleton is composed of parts that are 'indiarubbery', the cartilages; of parts that are somewhat elastic, such as the breast bone (the sternum), which is partly cartilaginous; as well as of bones that are hard. In the hock joint, the thrust of hard bone on hard bone is relieved by its being made up of several bones tightly bound together by strong ligaments; they form a mass rigid for all practical purposes, but not rigid as a single unit of bone is, and excessive shock is averted, because the component bones must undergo a compression before the force exerted on the hock (calcaneum) is transmitted to the cannon bone.

Variety of Joints It is very interesting to observe the variety of construction in the joints of a horse's leg which adapts them to different mechanical duties, so that, at any moment, whatever the strain to which the leg is subjected, there is always a specialist prepared to deal with it.

Thus, only one joint in each leg has freedom of movement in all directions, the other joints being practically limited to oscillation in a plane, whatever their other capacities.

In the fore leg the free-moving joint is the scapulo-humeral articulation, which corresponds to our shoulder joint. In the hind leg the free-moving joint is the coxa-femoral articulation, which corresponds to our hip joint; so similar indeed are the hip joints of man and horse that you may see a horse standing with one hind foot crossed over the other, much as a man often stands.

It is interesting to notice that, though they are both socket and ball joints, there is a distinct difference in the way in which they are articulated. As the sketches show, the socket of the hip joint is deep, especially towards the front of the leg, enclosing a large portion of the head of the femur; in the shoulder joint, the cup on the end of the shoulder blade (the

Ball and Socket Joints

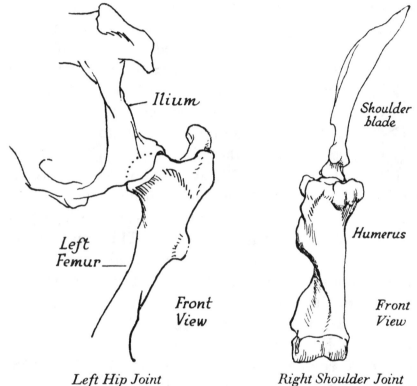

Left Hip Joint   *Right Shoulder Joint*

Glenoid cavity) is very small. These differences of construction are adapted to the principal duties of the hind and fore legs, the former making for firmness of attachment, the latter for great freedom of movement.

One joint with universal movement placed high on the leg is sufficient to allow the leg to swing forwards, backwards and outwards from the body with all the freedom that it needs, as when a horse is galloping on a curve, while the restriction of movement of the other joints gives the leg rigidity and strength.

E   L.T.H

Hinges   Below the ball and socket joints we get powerful straightforward articulations, the elbow and knee, stifle and hock, the

Left Hock
Inside View

knee and hock being shock absorbers with their layers of several bones, though otherwise unlike each other (see Pl. 6, p. 62; and Pl. 9, p. 82; also the astragalus on p. 28). In the hock the component bones are tied into an inseparable mass; in the knee they are knit so that they can open. For the knee (the carpus) is a joint made for the easy lifting of the fore leg, to prevent stumbling and for clearing obstacles as in jumping. The flexion of the joint is so free, from its being made with layers of bones which even slide a little upon each other, that a horse can flick his chest with his hoof to dislodge a fly that is teasing him. This construction of the knee moreover facilitates the action of the tendons that run across its surface; for, when the knee is bent, it offers them only slight changes of direction from the facets of one layer of bone to those of the next, instead of a harsh change of direction as a single-jointed hinge would do. When a horse falls, this opening of the bones makes the injury to the knee often very severe.

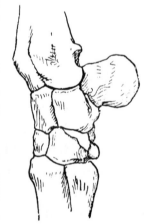

Left "Knee"
Outside View

The Knee   The sketches on p. 46 were made from X-ray photographs of the knee of a foal, taken from the inside. The proportion of the bones and their shape differ considerably from those of a mature horse, but the principle of movement is the same. The opening takes place first between the Radius and the

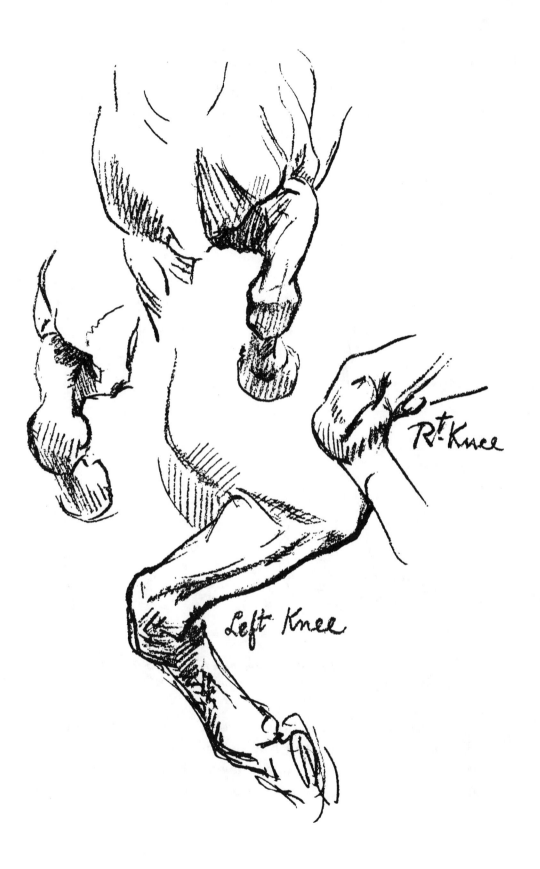

The Knee upper layer of carpal bones, later the hinge movement between the upper and lower layers of carpals becomes very large.

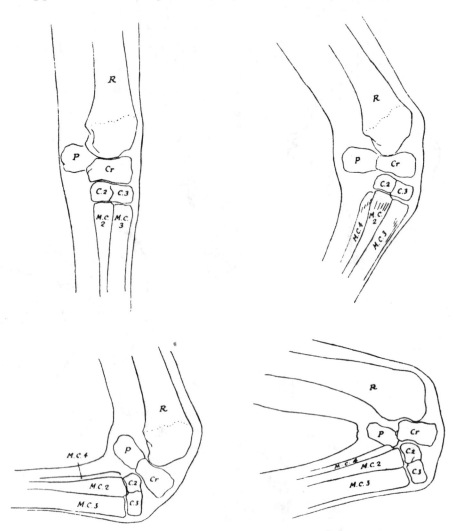

From X-ray photographs of a foal's left knee taken from the inside. Cr, C2, C3 = Carpal bones; MC = Metacarpals; MC3 = Cannon bone; MC2, MC4 = Splint bones; P = Pisiform bone; R = Radius.

A noticeable point is how, as soon as the knee bends, the Pisiform bone deserts the Radius and remains in the middle of the joint. Really the upper layer of carpal bones is the central platform of the knee on which turn first the Radius and later the lower row of carpals, which practically form a knob at the top of the cannon bone.

The Knee

As the stifle and hock, the big propulsive hinges of the equine motor, are linked together and work in unison (see Pl. 11, p. 108), all the tremendous power of the quarters is transmitted to the long lever of the hock, throwing tremendous strain upon the joint. To direct this force the double wheel of the astragalus is deeply embedded in grooves at the base of the tibia. This is a joint for the direct transmission of thrust. It is no joint for sideway strain, having no sideway play. Of that it must be relieved, as it is, by the play of the head of the femur in its socket above, and below by the elasticity of the pastern joints and hoof.

Union of Hock and Stifle

In the pasterns we find automatic springs, real spring shackles, so well designed that one foot can support the full weight of the body, taking the irregularities of the ground as they come. Firmly tied by ligaments against lateral displacement, their articulation with the cannon bone and each other is necessarily shallow; they would break if one bone was inserted in another, as in the hock. The pasterns have a very long swing to and fro. They can be flexed back at right angles to the cannon bone, and, supported by the tendons, can be extended forwards, 'overextended', not only into the position they occupy when a horse is standing at rest, but at times actually at right angles to the cannon bone.

Springs

The more one looks at the body the more one sees how interdependent the parts are, saving each other and complementing each other mechanically, complementing each other also in beauty and design, hard parts and soft, long and short, square and round, in contrast and repetition.

The attached impressions of fore leg and hind leg were rapidly drawn from a horse pulling very hard. They show clearly that the impression produced upon the eye was that the force of the muscles was directed to the joints.

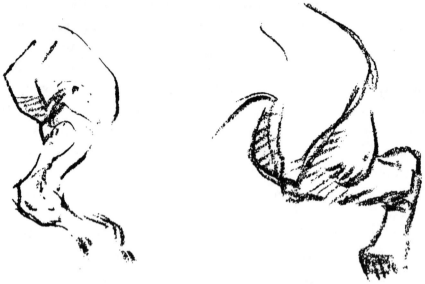

Left fore leg and hind leg pulling.

In drawing the fore leg the eye was caught by the squareness of the point of the shoulder, the angles of the knee and the swelling of the extensor muscles.

The sketch of the hind leg, if you will 'read' it carefully, shows the Vasti muscles (79) on the top and both sides of the femur concentrating on the knee-cap, the Biceps (70) swelling with the effort, and the line made by the Tendo Achillis (80*b*) running to the hock. It is noticeable, too, how squarely the foot is turned down, so that the toe digs into the ground.

When a horse is pulling really hard he lowers his forehand in order to put his hind legs into the position in which they get their thrust most directly into the line of the resistance. In fact, the horse lies down to it, as a man does when pulling in a tug-of-war. To do this he flexes his fore leg at elbow and knee joints, using his extensor muscles to keep his knee from closing altogether, which accounts for their accentuation in the sketch. As his flexors are pulling the foot back, one sees that in violent efforts the muscles on both sides of the leg are in action at *Fore and* once, which braces the leg and supports the bone against the *Hind Legs* severe strain that it is undergoing. The wheeler of a cart who has the weight of the shafts on him dare not 'lie down' to it, as a leader can with only traces upon him.

In the second sketch, of right and left fore legs seen from behind, it is again noticeable how the bone forms are em-

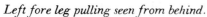

Left fore leg pulling seen from behind. *Right fore leg pulling seen from behind.*

phasized at the elbow and knee, and the foot is putting its toe into the ground. See also the drawing of knees on p. 34.

Which observations show how much the skeleton, hidden as it is, influences the superficial appearance of the body.

Chapter IV. The Muscles

'Muscles are highly specialized organs that have the property of contracting when stimulated. Striated muscles', the kind of muscles with which we are concerned, 'act upon the bones, cover the greater part of the skeleton and play an important part in determining the form of the animal.'[1]

Thus the voice of science, Sisson, *The Anatomy of the Domestic Animals.*

The muscles are attached to the bones either directly, or indirectly through the cartilages, ligaments or fascia. In the plates the areas of attachment marked upon the bones often represent only part of the attachment of a muscle which through fascia or aponeurosis applies its force to a much larger area of the bone or bones concerned.

The muscles cannot push the bones since they only work by contraction; so that when we push something our action is the result of pulling on the part of the muscles.

In the notes on the muscles, their action is described as extending or flexing a joint, or they are said to adduct, abduct, or rotate a limb inwards or outwards. While such terms conveniently express the action of a muscle, it should be remembered that the muscle which flexes a joint is also used to control its extension, just as one which extends it is used to control its flexion. For instance, when you jump, you employ the big muscles in the top of your thigh to straighten, to extend, your knee joint, and your calf muscles to extend your ankle joint; and when you land, the same muscles check the flexion

[1] As many people seem not to know it, let me mention that muscles are the flesh, or meat.

50

of your knee and ankle, and let you down gradually without shock. Your biceps, with which you lift a weight in your hand, also controls the delicacy with which you put it down again. The Adductors of a limb are as often used to control its outward swing as actually to pull it inwards. Indeed, the interplay of muscles even in a simple movement is very intricate; which is why a child takes some time before it can co-ordinate its movements, and why we find it difficult to learn new combinations of movements as in games.

Variety of Muscular Action

Muscles are as varied as the bones they serve, thick, thin, flat, round, long, short. In some the contraction makes no change of shape noticeable enough to concern the draughtsman, in others the change is very striking, as in the human biceps, as every schoolboy knows. Does the boy exist who has not clenched his fist and bent his arm hoping that his biceps will become an enormous ball of iron?

Muscles vary as much in their speed of action as in their strength, those with a long purchase starting a movement more easily than can those with a short leverage, though the latter make up in speed what they lack in initiative. To extend the femur on the pelvis, as in kicking, the muscles of the croup, Biceps femoris (70), Semimembranosus (72), and others, start the movement easily, for their pull is exerted at some distance from the fulcrum, the hip joint; but the Middle Glutæus (68a), with its pull on the short leverage of the great trochanter, adds a rapidity to the movement of the femur of which the others are incapable. A similar principle is employed by a man swinging an axe, who holds it near the blade to start the swing, and runs his hand down the haft to add speed to the finish of the stroke.

A point of interest is the difference of action in a muscle that connects one bone to the next, and of a muscle that, ignoring the next bone, passes to a bone beyond. The Brachialis (49), for instance, which arises on the humerus and is inserted on the radius, can only flex the elbow joint; while its neighbour the Biceps Brachii (47), which arises from the shoulder blade and passing by the humerus is also inserted on the radius, can flex the elbow joint if the shoulder is fixed, can extend the shoulder joint if the elbow is fixed, or carry out both functions simultaneously.

The flow of muscular action is clearly illustrated on the neck of a walking horse by the Serratus Cervicis (39*a*). Watch when the foot takes the ground and you will see, as the shoulder blade turns, the different strands of the muscle stand out in turn upon the neck, like a series of fingers, beginning with the strand which is nearest to the shoulder until they are all taut; see the illustration on p. 31.

The action of a muscle, however rapid, however instantaneous it appears, necessarily develops and diminishes gradually, as is noticeably shown in a slowed-down film in the cinematograph. This crescendo and diminuendo movement takes place not only in the action of an individual muscle, but also in the way in which muscles follow and combine with each other's actions. And when the crescendo and diminuendo is rhythmic it gives us pleasure through our eyes and we call it graceful.

*Description
of the
Muscles* In the descriptive lists, that follow, the muscles are numbered for convenience of reference; and the numbers appear on the plates with the name of the muscle. Sometimes for want of space on the plate the name of a muscle is abbreviated.

A muscle and its areas of origin or insertion on the bones bear the same colour on every plate in which they appear, and in the list this colour is noted against the muscle. The reader is warned, however, that in looking up certain of the plate references he may find only the area of attachment of the muscle to the bone, and not the muscle itself; of certain unimportant muscles only the attachment is given.

The names of the muscles are given as far as possible in English. Muscles have a great variety of names in different text-books, so much so that if the reader studies the subject further he will find, to his great inconvenience, that different authors use different names without mentioning the alternative names at all!

The description of the muscles is deliberately simplified. Often only the principal attachment or insertion is given, and only the principal functions mentioned. For simplicity's sake the Ligaments, a very interesting part of the mechanism of the joints, are hardly mentioned. Like other parts of the body the muscles are so intricate in structure, sharing their neighbours' attachments and duties, even at times acting in contradictory ways, that a full description would plunge the reader into the maze of technical terms that is called a text-book.

The action of most of the muscles of the head and face is clear from the plate without much explanation (see Pl. 1, p. 12).

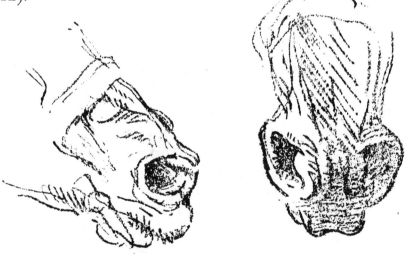

Those of which the contraction shows most are the big *Masseter muscles*, which as a horse munches tighten into ridges that radiate like the ribs of a fan, and the *Buccinator*, which forms the cheek just behind the mouth, opposite the teeth.

Though the muscles that move the nose, ears and eyelids are hardly ever noticeable in themselves, their influence on expression is great.

A horse pinches his nostrils and lays back his ears to show temper; blows through his nostrils when alarmed; and opens

them like trumpets when excited or galloping, for he does not breathe through his mouth. Horse races are run with closed lips, as men's races are run with open ones. He opens his mouth when he neighs.

A horse gets much information through his nose, for the long hairs with their sensitive roots are true feelers and he misses them if they are cut short, as they are sometimes, to 'make him look smarter'.

In his book, *The Anatomy of Expression*, Sir Charles Bell states that the muscles which in the lion lift the lips off the canine teeth, in the horse pass to the nose. The lion and the other felines can open the jaw right back to seize and chew their prey, while the horse can only open his mouth moderately; which must make it most uncomfortable when he yawns, but makes his mouth the better container to hold a quantity of fodder while he chews it.

Descriptive List of Muscles

[The plates in which the muscles are best shown are numbered in heavier type.]

1. *Orbicular of the Mouth* (*Orbicularis Oris*). Blue. Pl. 1.
   The sphincter of the mouth which closes the lips.

2. *Levator of the Upper Lip and Nostril* (*L. nasi labialis*). Red. Pl. 1.
   It lifts the upper lip and dilates the nostril.

3. *Levator of the Upper Lip* (*L. labii superioris proprius*). Mauve. Pl. 1.
   Working on each side of the face these muscles meet on the top of the nose, and acting together lift the upper lip, and can actually turn it inside out, as may be seen from time to time. Acting separately, they pull it sideways.

Levator of the Upper Lip

4. *Zygomaticus*. Green. Pl. 1.
   A thin ribbon which pulls back the corner of the mouth.

5. *Depressor of the Lower Lip* (*D. labii inferioris*). Red. Pl. 1.
   It pulls the lower lip backwards and downwards.

6. *Buccinator*. Mauve. Pl. 1.
   This muscle lies along the mouth. It is called the 'Trumpeter' because it tenses the sides of the mouth; it assists in pushing the food between the teeth in mastication.

7. *Masseter*. Yellow. Pl. 1.
   From the zygomatic arch and the crest to the lower jaw. This muscle closes the jaw when working in unison with its fellow on the other side of the head, or pulls it sideways as in mastication, when acting alone. It makes the

shape of the lower edge of the jaw. Its fan-shaped fibres show very distinctly when a horse is munching.

8. *Lateral Dilator of the Nose* (*Caninus muscle*). Yellow. Pl. 1.
It dilates the nostril.

9. *Superior Dilator of the Nose*. Green. Pl. 1.
It helps to enlarge the nasal cavity.

10. *Transverse Dilator of the Nose*. Yellow. Pl. 1.
Lies under the common tendon of the Levator of the Upper Lip (3).

11. *Cervical Ligament* (*Ligamentum Nuchae*). Buff. Pls. 1, 2.
It is an arrangement of elastic tissue to support the weight of the neck. It is composed of two parts, the funicular part, which arising from the withers is inserted into the occipital protuberance of the skull, and the lamellar part, which arising from the funicular part as well as from the withers is inserted into the 2nd to the 6th cervical vertebræ.

12. *Sterno-Cephalicus* (*Sterno-Mandibularis*). Yellow. Pls. 1, 2, 3, 10.
From the cartilage of the sternum to the angle of the lower jaw.
Action: Flexes the head and neck.

13. *Longus Colli*. Blue. Pl. 1.
It runs from the atlas bone along the underside of the neck to the 6th vertebra of the thorax, binding the vertebræ to each other.

14. *Intertransversales colli*. Green, clear and shaded. Pl. 1.
Attach the cervical vertebræ to each other, the clear and shaded areas of muscle interconnecting respectively.

15a. *Sterno-Thyro-Hyoideus*. Blue. Pl. 10.

15b. *Omo-Hyoideus.* Mauve. Pls. 1, 2, 3, 10.

These are two muscles, arising on the cariniform cartilage of the sternum and the subscapular fascia respectively, to be inserted on the hyoid bone, between the jaw bones; the thyroid branch of 15a is inserted on the larynx. They show in the throat, between the two branches of the sterno-cephalic muscle (12).

16. *Cutaneous muscle (Panniculus Carnosus).*

It adheres closely to the skin on certain parts of the body, the face, neck, arm and abdomen. It is the twitching muscle that dislodges insects.

16a. *Cutaneous of the Neck.* Green. Pls. 3, 10.

It arises in the sternum and the two parts diverge over the sterno-cephalic muscle to join the mastoido-humeralis, where it is gradually lost.

16b. *Cutaneous of the Abdomen.*

It covers a large part of the abdomen and flank.

17. *Rectus Capitis (Anticus Major.)* Yellow. Pls. 1, 2.

From the 3rd, 4th and 5th cervical vertebræ to the occipital bone. Action: Flexes or inclines the head.

18a. *Trapezius Cervical part.* Blue. Pls. 1, 3, 4, 5.

18b. *Trapezius Dorsal or Thoracic part.* Blue. Pls. 3, 4, 5.

From the cervical ligament and the withers to the spine of the shoulder blade, where it is divided into two parts. Action: The cervical part draws the shoulder blade forwards and upwards; the dorsal part draws it upwards and backwards. Acting together they lift the scapula.

The tendinous fibres that form the middle part of this muscle support the shoulder blade and fore limb when the leg is off the ground just as the tendinous fibres of the Serratus Thoracis support the fore parts of the body from the shoulder blade when the leg is on the ground (see p. 10).

Plate 5. Muscular Attachment of the Shoulder to the Body

[The numbers printed after the names of muscles are the numbers of the other plates in which the muscles appear.
The plates in which the muscles are best shown are numbered in heavier type.]

Numbers
and Colours
of the Muscles

16a. Green   *Cutaneous of the neck.* Pl. 3, 10.
18a. Blue   *Trapezius, Cervical part.* Pl. 1, 3, 4.
18b. Blue   *Trapezius, Dorsal part.* Pl. 3, 4.
32. Green   *Rhomboideus.* Pl. 2, 3, 4.
33. Green   *Latissimus Dorsi.* Pl. 3, 4, 10.
34. Red   *Mastoido-Humeralis.* Pl. 1, 3, 4, 10.
35. Yellow   *Anterior Superficial Pectoral.* Pl. 2, 3, 10.

Numbers
and Colours
of the Muscles

36. Blue   *Posterior Superficial Pectoral.* Pl. 6, 10.
37. Green   *Anterior Deep Pectoral.* Pl. 2, 4, 10.
38. Red   *Posterior Deep Pectoral.* Pl. 2, 3, 4, 10.
39a. Mauve   *Serratus Cervicis.* Pl. 1, 2, 3, 4.
39b. Mauve   *Serratus Thoracis.* Pl. 2, 3, 4, 11.

5

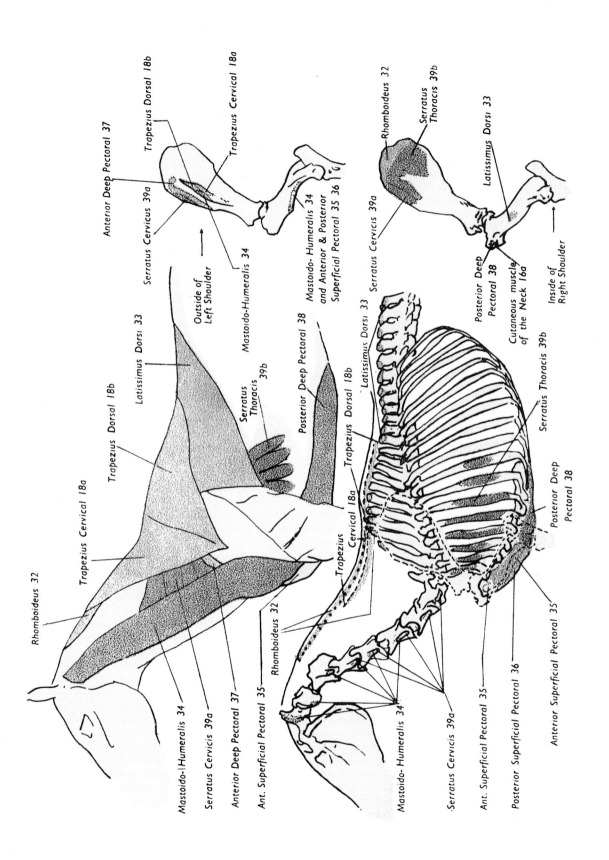

Rhomboideus 32

Trapezius Cervical 18a

Trapezius Dorsal 18b

Latissimus Dorsi 33

Mastoido-\Humeralis 34

Serratus Cervicis 39a

Anterior Deep Pectoral 37

Ant. Superficial Pectoral 35

Anterior Deep Pectoral 37

Trapezius Dorsal 18b

Trapezius Cervical 18a

Serratus Cervicis 39a

Outside of
Left Shoulder

Mastoido-Humeralis 34

Mastoido- Humeralis 34
and Anterior & Posterior
Superficial Pectoral 35 36

Serratus Cervicis 39a

Serratus
Thoracis
39b

Posterior Deep Pectoral 38

Rhomboideus 32

Serratus
Thoracis 39b

Latissimus Dorsi 33

Serratus Cervicis 39a

Posterior Deep
Pectoral 38

Cutaneous muscle
of the Neck 16a

Inside of
Right Shoulder

Latissimus Dorsi 33

Trapezius Dorsal 18b

Trapezius
Cervical 18a

Rhomboideus 32

Serratus Thoracis 39b

Posterior Deep
Pectoral 38

Mastoido-Humeralis 34

Serratus Cervicis 39a

Ant. Superficial Pectoral 35

Posterior Superficial Pectoral 36

Anterior Superficial Pectoral 35

19. *Splenius.* Yellow. Pls. 1, 3, 10.
From the 2nd, 3rd and 4th thoracic spines and the cervical ligament to the skull, atlas, and 3rd, 4th and 5th cervical vertebræ.
Action: To pull the head and neck to the side; or acting together to raise the head and neck.

20. *Longissimus capitis et atlantis.* Blue, Yellow. Pl. 2.
From the 1st and 2nd thoracic vertebræ to the base of the skull and wing of the atlas, respectively.
Action: To extend the head and neck, or acting singly to bend the head and neck.
They show at moments of strain.

21. *Complexus.* Red. Pl.2; attachments. Pl.1.
From 2nd, 3rd and 4th thoracic spines, the 1st to 6th thoracic vertebræ and the cervical vertebræ to the occipital bone.
Action: Strong extensors of the head and neck. Acting on one side only, incline the head and neck to the side.

22. *Multifidus Cervicis (Transverse Spinous muscle of the neck).* Red. Pl. 2.
From the articular processes of the last five cervical vertebræ to the spines of the preceding cervical vertebræ.
Action: It binds the neck together and extends it or flexes it.

23. *Posterior Oblique of the Head.* Mauve. Pls. 1, 2.
A short thick muscle which connects the atlas and axis bones. It is hidden under the Mastoido-Humeralis muscle (34).
Action: Rotates the atlas and head on the axis or holds axis still on the atlas.

24. *Anterior Oblique of the Head.* Green. Pl. 1.
It joins the atlas bone to the skull. Extends the skull, or flexes it laterally. It also is hidden.

F   L.T.H.

25a. Serratus Posterior (S. Exspiratorius). Mauve. Pls. 2, 3.
Helps in expiration.

25b. External Intercostals. Red. Pls. 2, 3.
Join the ribs to each other.

26. *Transversalis Costarum (Ilio-costalis).* Yellow. Pl. 2.
It lies alongside the Longissimus Dorsi from the lumbar
region to the 5th, 6th and 7th cervical vertebræ. It
helps to connect the back, ribs, etc.
Action: Extends the spine, or flexes it sideways and helps
in inspiration.

27. *Longissimus Dorsi.* Red. Pls. 2, 8 *including the*

27a. Spinalis. Red. Pl. 2.
The longest muscle in the body, extending from the sacrum and ilium to the last four cervical vertebræ; the
Middle Glutæus (68) gains power from being attached to
its aponeurosis. It lies upon upper surfaces of the ribs
against the spines of the backbone and forms the shape
of the back.
Action: It is a very powerful extensor of the back and
loins, aiding in all movements of the hind quarters,
such as kicking, pulling, jumping, rearing. Acting
on one side of the body only it flexes the spine sideways.

28. *Multifidus Dorsi.* Hidden.
It runs from the sacrum to the neck, hidden by the
Longissimus Dorsi (27). It is composed of bundles
which slope upwards and forwards, joining the processes
of the vertebræ together. It extends the spine.

29. *The Abdominal Tunic.* Buff. Pl. 10.
It is a sheet of elastic tissue which helps the muscles to
support the abdomen. Its upper layer covers the External oblique of the Abdomen (30a).

30a. *External Oblique of the Abdomen.* Green. Pls. 2, 3, 7, 8, 10.

Its origins are the last fourteen ribs, the lumbo-dorsal fascia and the tuber coxæ. Its broad aponeurosis, the fibres of which blend with those of the Internal oblique, covers the abdomen, and joins, at the linea alba, the aponeurosis of the same muscles of the other side of the body; with the Internal oblique, the Rectus abdominis and Abdominal Tunic it supports the abdomen.

Action: It compresses the abdomen and the internal organs. Acting singly it bends the body sideways; acting together these muscles arch the back.

30b. *Internal Oblique of the Abdomen.* Blue. Pls. 2, 8.

It lies underneath the preceding muscle. From the tuber coxæ it spreads like a fan to be inserted into the last four ribs and to mix its fibres with those of the External oblique.

Its action is similar to that of the External oblique.

31. *Rectus Abdominis.* Hidden. Attachment Red. Pl. 8.

This muscle, which arises on the breast bone and the adjacent ribs, is connected to the pubis.

Action: It helps to carry the weight of the abdomen, with the External (30a) and Internal (30b) oblique muscle and the Abdominal Tunic (29).

Action: Similar to that of the above muscles; arches the loins.

32. *Rhomboideus (Cervicalis and Thoracalis).* Green. Pls. 2, 3, 4, 5.

From the Ligamentum nuchae, and the spines of the 2nd to 7th thoracic vertebræ, to the underside of the cartilage of the shoulder blade.

Action: It draws the scapula upwards and forwards, or can raise the neck.

Plate 6. Bones and Muscles of the Fore Leg

[*The numbers printed after the names of muscles are the numbers of the other plates in which the muscles appear. The plates in which the muscles are best shown are numbered in heavier type.*]

*Numbers
and Colours
of the Muscles*

36. Blue   *Posterior Superficial Pectoral*. Pl. 5, **10**.
47. Green   *Biceps brachii (Coraco-radialis).*
               Pl. **2**, 4, 10, 11.
49. Blue   *Brachialis Anticus*. Pl. 2, 3, **4**, 10.
50. Mauve   *Tensor fascia antibrachii*. Pl. **4**, 10.
51a.⎫ Yellow   *Triceps brachii*. Pl. **2**, 3, 4.
51b.⎭
51c. Yellow   *Triceps Brachii* (Internal head). Pl **4**.
52. Red   *Anconeus*. Pl. **4**, 11.
53. Mauve   *External Radial Extensor (Ext. carpi
               radialis)*. Pl. 2, 3, **4**, 10, 11.
54. Green   *Common Digital Extensor (Ext. pedis).*
               Pl. 2, 3, **4**, 10, 11.
55. Yellow   *Laretal digital Extensor (Ext. Digiti
               Quinti)*. Pl. 2, 3, **4**, 10.

*Numbers
and Colours
of the Muscles*

56. Red   *Oblique Extensor of the Metacarpus
               (Abductor pollicis)*. Pl. **4**.
57. Yellow   *Internal Radial Flexor (Fx. Carpi
               radialis)*. Pl. **4**.
58. Green   *Middle Flexor of the Metacarpus
               (Fx. carpi ulnaris)*. Pl. **4**.
59. Blue   *External Flexor of the Metacarpus
               (Ulnaris lateralis)*. Pl. 2, 3, **4**, 10.
60. Red   *Superficial digital Flexor (Perforatus)
               and check ligament*. Pl. **4**, 11.
61. Mauve   *Deep Digital Flexor (Perforans) and
               check ligament*. Pl. **4**, 11.
62. Blue   *Suspensory Ligament*. Pl. 11.
67. Yellow   *Internal Radial Flexor (Fx. carpi
               radialis)*. Pl. **4**.

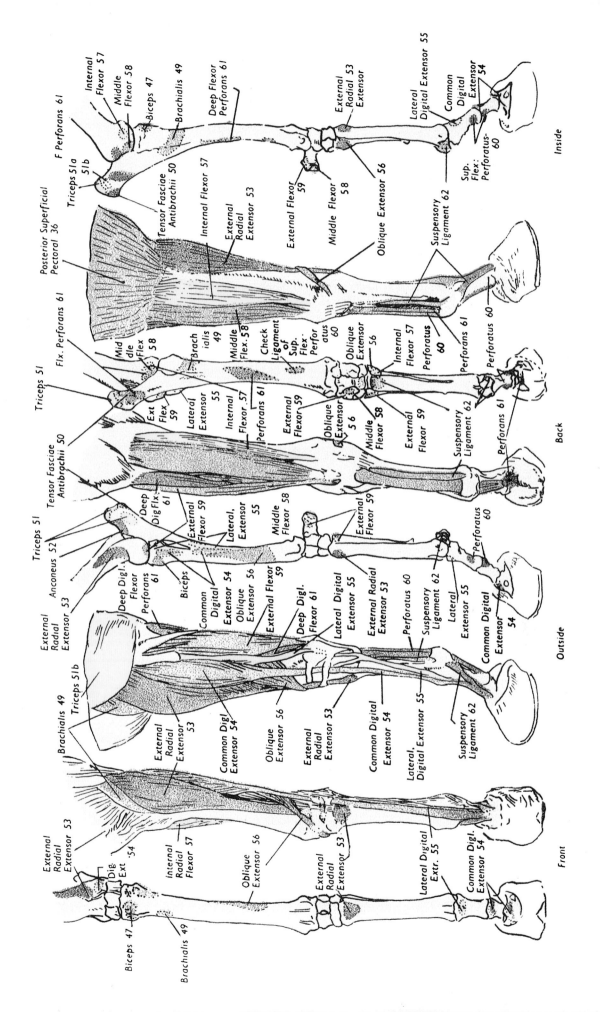

6

Inside

Internal Flexor 57
Middle Flexor 58
Biceps 47
Brachialis 49
Deep Flexor Perforans 61
External Radial 53 Extensor
Lateral Digital Extensor 55
Common Digital Extensor 54
F Perforans 61
Triceps 51a 51b
Tensor Fasciae Antibrachii 50
Internal Flexor 57
External Radial Extensor 53
External Flexor 59
Middle Flexor 58
Oblique Extensor 56
Sup. Flex: Perforatus 60

Posterior Superficial Pectoral 36
Suspensory Ligament 62
Perforans 61
Perforatus 60

Back

Triceps 51
Flx. Perforans 61
Middle Flex 58
Brach ialis 49
Middle Flex. 58
Check Ligament of Sup. Flex. Perfor atus 60
Oblique Extensor 56
Internal Flexor 57
Perforatus 60
Perforans 61

Ext Flex 59
Lateral Extensor 55
Internal Flexor 57
Perforans 61
External Flexor 59
Oblique Extensor 56
Middle Flexor 58
External Flexor 59
Suspensory Ligament 62
Perforans 61

Tensor Fasciae Antibrachii 50
Triceps 51

Outside

Triceps 51
Anconeus 52
External Radial Extensor 53
Deep Digl. Flexor Perforans 61
Biceps
Common Digital Extensor 54
Oblique Extensor 56
External Flexor 59
Deep Digl. Flexor 61
Lateral Digital Extensor 55
External Radial Extensor 53
Perforatus 60
Suspensory Ligament 62
Lateral Extensor 55
Common Digital Extensor 54

Deep Digl. Flexor 61
Lateral, Extensor 55
Middle Flexor 58
External Flexor 59

Brachialis 49
Triceps 51b
External Radial Extensor 53
Common Digl Extensor 54
Oblique Extensor 56
External Radial Extensor 53
Common Digital Extensor 54
Lateral, Digital Extensor 55
Suspensory Ligament 62

Front

External Radial Extensor 53
Dig. Ext. 54
Internal Radial Flexor 57
Oblique Extensor 56
External Radial Extensor 53
Lateral Digital Extr. 55
Common Digl. Extensor 54

Biceps 47
Brachialis 49

33. *Latissimus Dorsi.* Green. Pls. 3, 4, 5, 10.
From the lumbo-dorsal fascia to the tubercle on the under-side of the humerus. It overlaps the edge of the scapula.
Action: It is a powerful agent in the action of the front leg. Pulling the humerus upwards and backwards, or equally pulling the body forwards. It also tends to flex the shoulder joint.

34. *Mastoido-humeralis* (or *Brachio-cephalicus*). Red. Pls. 1, 3, 4, 5, 10.
From the deltoid tuberosity and the fascia covering the shoulder and humerus, to the skull (the mastoid and nuchal crest), the wing of the atlas bone, and the 2nd, 3rd and 4th cervical vertebræ.
Action: When the head and neck are fixed it pulls the fore limb forwards, extending the shoulder joint; when the limb is fixed, it extends the head and neck or inclines them. It also helps to extend the elbow through its pull upon the strong fascia from the deltoid tuberosity to the outer face of the elbow.

35. *Anterior Superficial Pectoral* (or *Pectoralis descendens*). Yellow. Pls. 2, 3, 5, 10.
From the prow of the sternum, to the humerus and fascia of the arm. These muscles form the very characteristic bosom-like form of the chest.
Action: To adduct and advance the limb.

36. *Posterior Superficial Pectoral* (or *Pectoralis transversus*). Blue. Pls. 5, 6, 10.
From the ventral edge of the sternum to the humerus, with the preceding muscle.
Action: Adducts the limb.

37. *Anterior Deep Pectoral* (*Sterno praescapularis*). Green. Pls. 2, 4, 5, 10.
Side of the sternum and first four ribs to the fascia of the Supraspinatus (41).

Action: To adduct the limb, and pull it backwards; equally to pull the body forwards when the leg is fixed.

38. *Posterior Deep Pectoral* (*Pectoralis ascendens*). **Red. Pls. 2, 3, 4, 5, 10.**

From the sternum, the fourth to ninth ribs, and abdominal tunic, to the tuberosity on the underside of the humerus and tendon of the coraco-brachialis.

Action: To adduct the limb, and pull it backwards; equally to pull the body forwards.

39a. *Serratus Cervicis.* Mauve. Pls. 1, 2, 3, 4, 5.

From the underside of the shoulder blade to the last four or five cervical vertebræ.

39b. *Serratus Thoracis.* Mauve. Pls. 2, 3, 4, 5, 11.

From the first eight or nine ribs to the underside of the shoulder blade.

Action: The cervical part draws the top of the scapula forwards; the thoracic part pulls it downwards. Acting together they raise the body in relation to the shoulder blade, and when at rest form a sort of sling supporting the body (see p. 11).

40. *Deltoid.* Mauve. Pls. 3, 4.

From the spine and the dorsal angle of the scapula and a tendinous insertion on its spine, to the deltoid tuberosity on the humerus.

Action: It flexes the shoulder joint, and abducts the humerus. When the fore leg is raised its tension produces a channel across the form of the shoulder.

41. *Supraspinatus.* Blue. Pls. 2, 4.

Fills the hollow on the shoulder blade, in front of the spine. It is inserted on the inner and outer side of the top of the humerus.

Action: Extends the joint and steadies it against strain and shock—see Subscapularis (44).

42. *Infraspinatus.* Red. Pls. 2, 4.

Fills the hollow behind the spine of the shoulder blade, and has a double insertion on the outer tuberosity of the humerus.

Action: Abducts and rotates the humerus. The action of this muscle is opposed by that of the Subscapularis; when working simultaneously they brace the joint. See Subscapularis (44).

43. *Teres Minor.* Green. Pls. 2, 4.

Its origin runs along the posterior edge of the Infraspinatus, and it is inserted on a knob just above the deltoid tuberosity of the humerus.

Action: Flexes, rotates and abducts the humerus.

44. *Subscapularis.* Yellow. Pl. 4.

Occupies most of the underside of the shoulder blade, and is inserted on the interior tuberosity of the humerus.

Action: It adducts the humerus—see Infraspinatus (42).

The shoulder blade is articulated with the humerus in a shallow ball and socket joint and is braced as well as rotated and flexed by the muscles on each side of it. There is a general balance of opposition between the Infraspinatus (42) and Supraspinatus (41) on one side and the Subscapularis (44) on the other.

45. *Teres Major.* Red. Pls. 4, 10.

From the dorsal angle of the shoulder blade to the tubercle on the inner side of the humerus, in common with the Latissimus Dorsi (33).

Action: Flexes the shoulder joint, and adducts the humerus.

46. *Coraco-brachialis.* Mauve. Pls. 4, 10.

From the coracoid process on the underside of the shoulder blade to the interior surface of the humerus.

Action: Adducts the arm, and flexes the shoulder joint.

47. *Biceps Brachii* (*Coraco-Radialis*). Green. Pls. 2, 4, 6, 10, 11.

From the coracoid process of the shoulder blade, it runs down in front of the humerus, riding on the ridges on the front of the humerus, which keep it in place.

It is inserted into the tuberosity of the radius. A stout tendinous band passes from it to the External Radial Extensor (53).

Action: To flex the elbow joint; or extend the shoulder joint; or it braces the joints—see a description of its action, pp. 11, 14, 15.

48a. *Capsularis Brachii*. Mauve. Pl. 4.

From the glenoid cavity on the underside of the shoulder blade to the posterior of the humerus. It is very small and hidden, and does not affect the surface forms.

48b. *Capsularis Femoris*. Mauve. Pls. 7, 8.

It does not affect the surface forms. The Capsularis muscles prevent the capsules from getting pinched in the shoulder and hip joints respectively.

49. *Brachialis Anticus*. Blue. Pls. 2, 3, 4, 6, 10.

It rises from the spiral groove on the humerus, and passing the lower end of the biceps is inserted on the inner tuberosity of the radius.

Action: It flexes the elbow joint and rotates the radius.

50. *Tensor Fasciae Antibrachii*. Mauve. Pls. 4, 6, 10.

It lies on the underside of the shoulder blade, arising from the posterior border of the shoulder blade and the tendon of the Latissimus Dorsi (33), and is inserted on the back of the elbow and the fascia of the forearm.

Action: It extends the elbow.

51. *Triceps Brachii*, Yellow, is divided into three parts :

51a. *Long Head* (*Caput Longum*). Yellow. Pls. 2, 3, 4, 6, 11.

The long head takes its rise from the dorsal angle and

the posterior edge of the shoulder blade, to be inserted on the olecranon.

51b. *External Head (Caput Laterale)*. Yellow. Pls. 2, 3, 4, 6, 11.

The external head takes its origin on the rough line on the outside of the humerus above the deltoid tubercle, and is inserted on the top of the olecranon with the long head.

51c. *Internal Head (Caput mediale)*. Yellow. Pls. 4, 6.

The internal head arises on the inside of the middle of the humerus, and is inserted on the inner side of the olecranon.

Action: They all three extend the elbow joint. See also, for their special actions, pp. 16, 17.

52. *Anconeus*. Red. Pls. 4, 6, 11.

It is covered by the triceps. It rises on the posterior part of the humerus, and is inserted on the olecranon below the triceps.

Action: A weak supporter of the last two muscles and also acts as a Capsularis.

53. *External Radial Extensor (Extensor carpi radialis)*. Mauve. Pls. 2, 3, 4, 6, 10, 11.

From the extensor condyle of the humerus and the fascia overlying the brachialis. Its tendon runs down the front of the radius and is attached to the tuberosity on the front of the cannon bone (large metacarpal bone).

Action: It is the most powerful extensor of the knee joint, or it can flex the elbow joint. This muscle receives the tendon from the biceps. See Biceps (47) and p. 11 for its action.

54. *Common Digital Extensor of the Fore Leg (Ext. Pedis)*. Green. Pls. 2, 3, 4, 6, 10, 11.

This muscle takes its origins on the humerus just below

the preceding muscle, on the radius and ulna, and the ligament of the elbow joint. Its long tendon, which crosses the knee outside the previous muscle, slopes across the cannon bone to be inserted in the front of the third phalanx, which is hidden in the hoof.

Action: It extends the digits and the knee, and can help to flex the elbow. In action, it stands out sharply.

55. *Lateral Digital Extensor (Extensor Digiti Quinti).* Yellow. Pls. 2, 3, 4, 6, 10.

Its origin is on the radius, the humerus and the external lateral ligament of the elbow joint. Its tendon, which passes down the outside of the knee, slopes forward below it, to be inserted on the front of the first phalanx.

Action: It extends the digit and the knee joint.

56. *Oblique Extensor of the Metacarpus (Abductor Pollicis).* Red. Pls. 4, 6.

Its origin is on the external side of the radius, under the two preceding muscles. Just above the knee it passes over the tendon of the External Radial muscle (53), to be inserted on the inside of the knee on the second metacarpal bone.

Action: It extends the knee, and rotates the leg outwards.

57. *Internal Radial Flexor (Fx. Carpi Radialis).* Yellow. Pls. 4, 6.

Originates from the lower end of the inside of the humerus, and is inserted just below the knee on the second metacarpal bone.

Action: It flexes the knee, or alternatively can extend the elbow joints.

58. *Middle Flexor of the Metacarpus (Fx. Carpi Ulnaris).* Green. Pls. 4, 6.

Its origins are on the inside of the humerus, just below

the preceding muscle, and on the olecranon, and its tendon is inserted on the pisiform bone.

Action: To flex the knee, or alternatively to extend the elbow joint.

59. *External Flexor of the Metacarpus* (*Ulnaris Lateralis*). Blue. Pls. 2, 3, 4, 6, 10.

Its origin is on the lower outside edge of the humerus; it has an insertion on the pisiform bone, and a continuation of it runs in a groove on that bone, to be inserted on the external splint bone (the fourth metacarpal).

Action: It flexes the knee and extends the elbow.

60. *Superficial Digital Flexor* (or *Perforatus*). Red. Pls. 4, 6, 11.

It is called 'Superficial' because of its tendon, which forms the back of the leg below the knee, for the muscle itself is hidden by the External Flexor (59), the Middle Flexor (58) and the Internal Flexor (57).

It arises from the lower edge of the inside of the humerus, and is joined by a fibrous band, which arising from the lower part of the back of the radius fuses with its tendon. Its tendon then passes down the back of the knee and cannon bone. Towards the bottom of the cannon bone, on a level with the sesamoid bones, the tendon forms a ring, through which the tendon of the Deep Flexor (61) passes. Hence its other name, 'Perforatus'. The tendon now divides into two parts, which pass on each side of the first phalanx, to be inserted on the second phalanx, just above the coronet.

Action: It flexes the digits, and the knee joints, or can help to extend the elbow joint. See p. 23 for the action of the fibrous band which acts as check tendon.

61. *Deep Digital Flexor* (or *Perforans*) *of the Fore Leg*. Mauve. Pls. 4, 6, 11.

It has the same origin on the humerus as the preceding muscle, also an origin in the ulna and on the radius.

Plate 7. Bones and Muscles of the Thigh : outside views

[The numbers printed after the names of muscles are the numbers of the other plates in which the muscles appear.
The plates in which the muscles are best shown are numbered in heavier type.]

Numbers
and Colours
of the Muscles

30a. Green External Oblique of the Abdomen. Pl. 2, 3, 8, 10.

48b. Mauve Capsularis. Pl. 8.

64. Yellow Ilio-psoas. Pl. 8.

64b. Yellow Iliacus. Pl. 2, 8.

66. Mauve Tensor fasciæ latæ. Pl. 3, 8, 11.

67. Blue Superficial Glutæus. Pl. 3, 8.

68a. Mauve Middle Glutæus. Pl. 2, 8, 11.

68b. Yellow Piriformis. Pl. 8.

69. Green Deep Glutæus. Pl. 8.

70. Red Biceps Femoris. Pl. 3, 8, 9, 11.

71. Green Semitendinosus. Pl. 2, 3, 8, 9, 11.

72. Blue Semimembranosus. Pl. 2, 8, 9, 11.

76. Mauve Adductor Femoris. Pl. 8, 9.

77a. Red Quadratus Femoris. Pl. 8.

78. Gemelli. Pl. 8.

Numbers
and Colours
of the Muscles

79a. Red Rectus Femoris. Pl. 2, 3, 8, 9, 11.

79b. Yellow External Vastus (V. lateralis). Pl. 2, 3, 8, 9, 11.

80a. Blue Gastrocnemius. Pl. 2, 3, 8, 9, 11.

80b. Blue Tendo Achillis. Pl. 11.

81. Red Soleus. Pl. 2, 3, 9, 11.

82. Red Peronæus Tertius. Pl. 8, 9, 11.

84. Green Anterior or Long Digital Extensor (Ext. pedis). Pl. 2, 3, 9, 11.

85. Yellow Lateral Digital Extensor. Pl. 2, 3, 9.

86. Red Superficial Digital Flexor (Perforatus). Pl. 8, 9, 11.

87. Mauve Deep Digital Flexor (Perforans). Pl. 2, 3, 9, 11.

88. Yellow Popliteus. Pl. 8, 9.

7

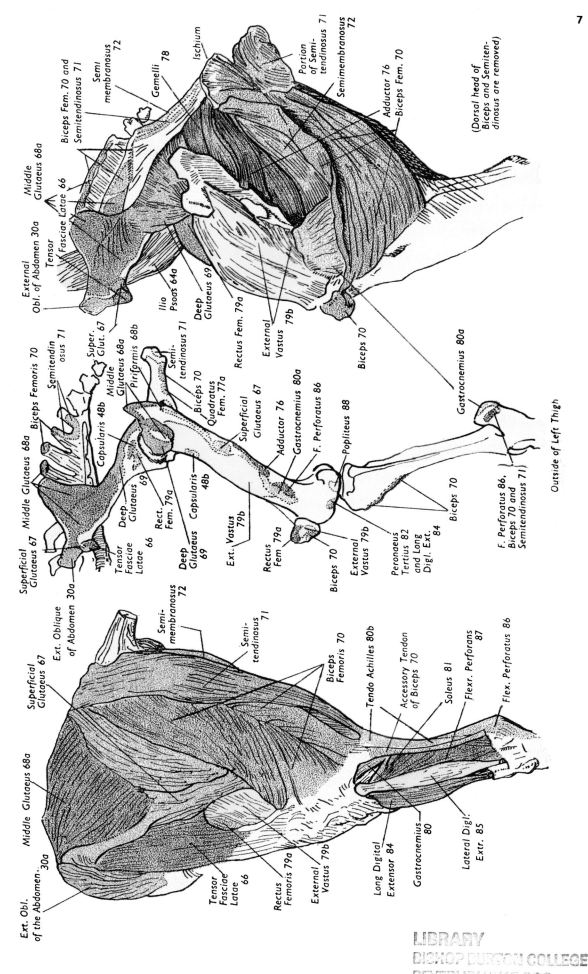

(Dorsal head of Biceps and Semitendinosus are removed)

Portion of Semitendinosus 71

Semimembranosus 72

Adductor 76

Biceps Fem. 70

Ischium

Gemelli

78

Biceps Fem. 70 and Semitendinosus 71

Semi membranosus 72

Middle Gluteaus 66

Tensor Fasciae Latae 66

External Obl. of Abdomen 30a

Ilio Psoas 64a

Deep Gluteaus 69

Rectus Fem. 79b

External Vastus 79b

Biceps 70

Gastrocnemius 80a

Outside of Left Thigh

Superficial Gluteaus 67

Middle Gluteaus 68a

Biceps Femoris 70

Semitendinosus 71

Super. Glut. 67

Capsularis 48b

Middle Gluteaus 68a

Piriformis 68b

Semitendinosus 71

Biceps 70

Quadratus Fem. 77a

Superficial Gluteaus 67

Adductor 76

Gastrocnemius 80a

F. Perforatus 86

Popliteus 88

Tensor Fasciae Latae 66

Deep Gluteaus 69

Rect. Fem. 79a

Deep Gluteaus 69

Capsularis 48b

Ext. Vastus 79b

Rectus Fem. 79a

Biceps 70

External Vastus 79b

Peronaeus Tertius 82 and Long Digl. Ext. 84

Biceps 70

F. Perforatus 86, Biceps 70 and Semitendinosus 71

Ext. Obl. of the Abdomen 30a

Middle Gluteaus 68a

Superficial Gluteaus 67

Ext. Oblique of Abdomen 30a

Semimembranosus 72

Semitendinosus 71

Biceps Femoris 70

Tendo Achilles 80b

Accessory Tendon of Biceps 70

Soleus 81

Flexr. Perforans 87

Flex. Perforatus 86

Tensor Fasciae Latae 66

Rectus Femoris 79a

External Vastus 79b

Long Digital Extensor 84

Gastrocnemius 80

Lateral Digl. Extr. 85

The tendon common to all its three heads passes the back of the knee and cannon bone; towards the middle of the latter it is joined by a 'check ligament'. Lower it passes through the ring in the preceding muscle, hence its name of Flexor Perforans, and is inserted within the hoof on the underside of the third phalanx, the coffin bone.

In the living horse it is very rarely possible to see the division between the Superficial and Deep Flexor tendons. The muscle of the Deep Flexor, which is not buried like the Superficial Flexor, shows above the knee between the Lateral Extensor (55) and the External Flexor (59) muscles.

Action: To flex the digits and the knee: it can alternatively help to extend the elbow joint.

For the action of the check tendon see p. 23.

62. *The Suspensory Ligament (Interosseus medius) of the Fore Leg.* Blue. Pls. 6, 11.

It has some muscular fibres and is extremely elastic, though it is almost entirely tendinous. In the fore leg it takes its origin at the back of the knee and at the top of the cannon bone, dividing into two strands which are inserted on the sesamoid bones of the fetlock. The tendon gives off a band on each side of the fetlock, which join the tendon of the common digital extensor.

Action: To support the fetlock, see p. 23; and compare the Suspensory Ligament of the Hind Leg (89).

63. *Psoas Minor.* Red. Pl. 8.

It connects the ilium to the lumbar and last two dorsal vertebræ.

Action: It flexes the pelvis on the loins.

64. *Ilio-Psoas.* Yellow. Pls. 7, 8. Composed of 64*a* and 64*b*.

64a. *Psoas Major.* Yellow. Pl. 8.

It lies on the ventral surface of the backbone, taking its origin from the 16th dorsal vertebra and the lumbar vertebræ; it is inserted on the inside of the femur, with the iliacus.

Action: It turns the femur outwards, and flexes the hip joint.

64b. *Iliacus.* Yellow. Pls. 2, 7, 8.

Originating under the ilium, on the sacrum and from the tendon of the Psoas Major, it is inserted with the latter on the inside of the femur. Owing to its close connection with the Psoas Major at their insertion, they are often considered as a single muscle, the Ilio-psoas.

Action: It also turns the femur outwards, and flexes the hip joint.

65. *Quadratus Lumborum.* Hidden. Red. Pl. 8.

It lies on the underside of the backbone; arising from the last two ribs and the lumbar transverse processes, it is inserted on the sacrum and the sacro-iliac ligament.

Action: Acting singly flexes the loins sideways.

66. *Tensor Fasciæ Latæ.* Mauve. Pls. 3, 7, 8, 11.

From the angle of the ilium to the Fascia lata it pulls on the knee-cap and the tibia.

Action: It tautens the Fascia lata; flexes the hip joint or extends the stifle. See p. 25.

67. *Superficial Glutæus.* Blue. Pls. 3, 7, 8.

From the external border of the ilium and gluteal fascia to the external trochanter of the femur.

Action: It pulls the femur forwards, rotating it inwards, and flexes the hip joint.

68a. *Middle Glutæus (Glutæus medius).* Mauve. Pls. 2, 7, 8, 11.

A very strong muscle, it is hidden by the fascia. From the external surface of the ilium and the aponeurosis of the

Longissimus Dorsi (27) to two insertions on the great trochanter of the thigh. Its attachment to the Longissimus Dorsi adds to its power, as in jumping, kicking, etc.

68b. *Piriformis.*   Yellow. Pls. 7, 8.
Hardly separable from the Middle Glutæus.

69. *Deep Glutæus.* Green. Pls. 7, 8.
Lies underneath the preceding muscle from the ilium to the great trochanter.
Action: Extends the hip joint, and abducts the thigh.

70. *Biceps femoris.* Red. Pls. 3, 7, 8, 9, 11.
It is a very powerful muscle with several insertions. Taking its origin from the sacrum, the gluteal fascia and the ischium, it sweeps down (*a*) to be inserted in the femur just behind the external trochanter, (*b*) to be attached to the patella, and (*c*) to the crest of the tibia and the fascia of the leg, while (*d*) a strong tendon branches off to be inserted on the tuber calcis, the tip of the hock. This tendon makes the characteristic contour of this part of the hind limb.
Action: It pulls the leg backwards and extends the limb generally. Its many points of attachment make its action complex. It extends the hock through the tendon (*d*); it also extends the femur in the pelvis and pulls back the femur and tibia simultaneously through the actions of the attachments *a*, *b* and *c*; see Pl. 11 and Ch. IX, p. 111.

71. *Semitendinosus.* Green. Pls. 2, 3, 7, 8, 9, 11.
It originates from the sacral and first caudal vertebræ, and from the ischium. It is attached, by a tendon passing internally, to the crest of the tibia and the fascia of the leg. It sends off a tendon which unites with that of the

Biceps (70), which is inserted in the tuber calcis of the hock.

Action : Its attachment to the tibia rotates the thigh inwards: flexes the stifle joint. It also helps in propulsion by pulling the leg in general backwards, thus extending the hock and hip joint. See Ch. IX, p. 111.

72. *Semimembranosus.* Blue. Pls. 2, 7, 8, 9, 11.

It originates from the underside of the ischium and also from the ligament that runs from the sacrum to the ischium. It lies under the Gracilis muscle (74) and its tendon is inserted on the inside of the lower end of the femur.

Action: Similar to and generally in unison with that of the Semitendinosus (71) and the Biceps (70).

73. *Sartorius.* Mauve. Pl. 8, 9.

From the iliac fascia under the pelvis to be inserted with the tendon of the Gracilis (74) on the inside of the patella, the tibia, and the fascia of the leg.

Action: It flexes the hip joint and adducts the femur.

74. *Gracilis.* Yellow. Pls. 8, 9.

Its origin is on the pelvic symphysis and under surface of the pubis. It is inserted on the patella and the fascia of the leg, and also with the previous muscle on the inner side of the tibia.

From behind, this muscle gives the characteristic square shape to the inside of the leg.

It opposes its power to that of the muscles on the outside of the thigh, much as the Subscapularis (44) on the underside of the shoulder blade opposes the muscles on its upper side.

Action: Adducts the femur.

75. *Pectineus.* Hidden. Red. Pl. 8.

It originates on the pubis and is inserted on the inside of

the femur half-way up; it is practically hidden by the Gracilis (74).

Action: It adducts the femur and flexes the hip.

76. *Adductor femoris*. Mauve. Pls. 7, 8, 9.
From the underside of the pelvis to the back of the femur, and to the stifle joint. It lies under the Gracilis (74). It adducts the femur, and extends the hip joint.

77a. *Quadratus Femoris*. Red. Pls. 7, 8.

77b. *Obturator, Externus*. Yellow. Pl. 8.

77c. *Obturator, Internus*. Mauve. Pl. 8.
There are several minor muscles, such as these and the next muscle, which reinforce the action of their more powerful neighbours, but do not concern the observer of the outside shapes of the body.

78. *Gemelli*. Red. Pls. 7, 8.
From the lateral border of the ischium to the fossa on the inside of the trochanter. They help to rotate the femur outwards.

79. *Quadriceps Femoris*.
This includes the four following muscles:

79a. *Rectus Femoris*. Red. Pls. 2, 3, 7, 8, 9, 11.
This muscle, which lies on the front of the thigh, takes its origin on the ilium; and has its tendon inserted on the knee-cap.
Action: It can extend the stifle joint, since the knee-cap is attached by a ligament to the tibia; it also flexes the hip joint, when the stifle is fixed; when the hind leg is lifted and coming forward for the next stride, its action brings the leg forward by simultaneously flexing the femur on the ilium, and extending the tibia on the femur.

G   L.T.H.

Plate 8. Bones and Muscles of the Thigh : inside and back views

[*The numbers printed after the names of muscles are the numbers of the other plates in which the muscles appear. The plates in which the muscles are best shown are numbered in heavier type.*]

Numbers and Colours of the Muscles

27.	Red	Longissimus Dorsi. Pl. 2.
30a.	Green	External Oblique of the Abdomen. Pl. 2, 3, 7, 10.
30b.	Blue	Internal Oblique of the Abdomen. Pl. 2.
31.	Red	Rectus Abdominis.
48b.	Mauve	Capsularis. Pl. 7.
63.	Red	Psoas Minor.
64.	Yellow	Ilio-Psoas. Pl. 7.
64a.	Yellow	Psoas Major.
64b.	Yellow	Iliacus. Pl. 2, 7.
65.	Red	Quadratus lumborum, attachment.
66.	Mauve	Tensor fasciæ latæ. Pl. 3, 7, 11.
67.	Blue	Superficial Glutæus. Pl. 3, 7.
68a.	Mauve	Middle Glutæus (G. Medius). Pl. 2, 7, 11.
68b.	Yellow	Piriformis. Pl. 7.
69.	Green	Deep Glutæus. Pl. 7.
70.	Red	Biceps Femoris. Pl. 3, 7, 9, 11.
71.	Green	Semitendinosus. Pl. 2, 3, 7, 9, 11.
72.	Blue	Semimembranosus. Pl. 2, 7, 9, 11.

Numbers and Colours of the Muscles

73.	Mauve	Sartorius. Pl. 9.
74.	Yellow	Gracilis. Pl. 9.
75.	Red	Pectineus.
76.	Mauve	Adductor Femoris. Pl. 7, 9.
77a.	Red	Quadratus Femoris. Pl. 7.
77b.	Yellow	Obturator Externus.
77c.	Mauve	Obturator Internus.
78.	Red	Gemelli. Pl. 7.
79a.	Red	Rectus Femoris. Pl. 2, 3, 7, 9, 11.
79b.	Yellow	External Vastus (V. Lateralis). Pl. 2, 3, 7, 9, 11.
79c.	Green	Internal Vastus (V. Medialis). Pl. 9.
80.	Blue	Gastrocnemius. Pl. 2, 3; 7, 9, 11.
82.	Red	Peronæus Tertius. Pl. 7, 9, 11.
84.	Green	Long Digital Extensor. Pl. 2, 3, 7, 9, 11.
85.	Yellow	Lateral Digital Extensor. Pl. 2, 3, 7, 9.
86.	Red	Perforatus. (Sup. Digital Fx.). Pl. 7, 9, 11.
88.	Yellow	Popliteus. Pl. 8, 9.
92b.	Blue	Jugular Vein.

8

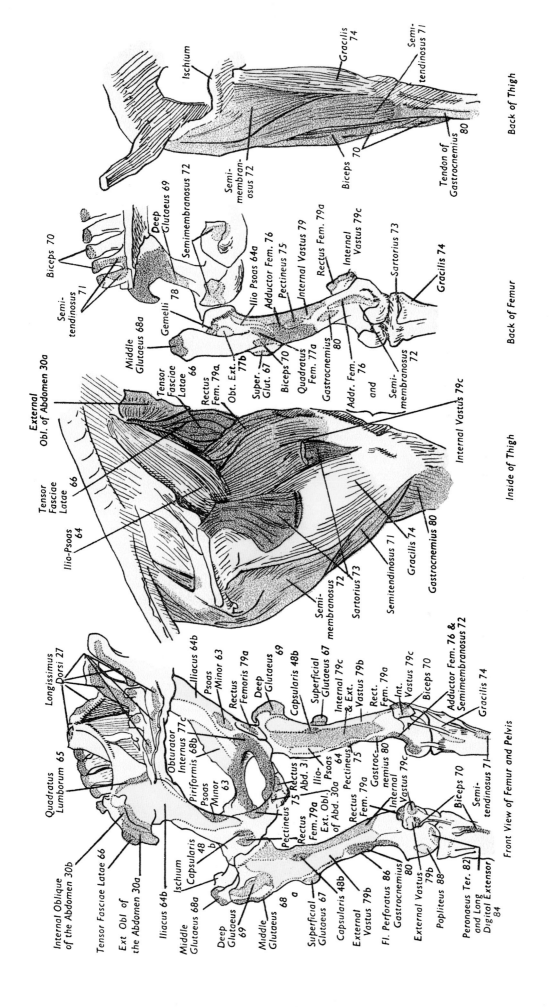

Back of Thigh

Gracilis 74

Semi-
tendinosus 71

Deep
Gluteaus 69

Semimembranosus 72

Semi-
membran-
osus 72

Biceps 70

Tendon of
Gastrocnemius 80

Ischium

Biceps 70

Semi-
tendinosus
71

Middle
Glutaeus 68a

Tensor Fasciae
Latae 66

Gemelli
78

Ilio Psoas 64a

Adductor Fem. 76

Pectineus 75

Internal Vastus 79

Rectus Fem. 79a

Internal
Vastus 79c

Sartorius 73

Gracilis 74

Rectus
Fem. 79a

Obt. Ext.
77b

Super.
Glut. 67

Biceps 70

Quadratus
Fem. 77a

Gastrocnemius
80

Addr. Fem.
76
and

Semi-
membranosus
72

Back of Femur

External
Obl. of Abdomen 30a

Tensor
Fasciae
Latae

Tensor
Fasciae
Latae
66

Ilio-Psoas
64

Semi-
membranosus
72

Sartorius 73

Semitendinosus 71

Gracilis 74

Gastrocnemius 80

Internal Vastus 79c

Inside of Thigh

Longissimus
Dorsi 27

Quadratus
Lumborum 65

Iliacus 64b

Psoas
Minor 63

Rectus
Femoris 79a

Deep
Glutaeus
69

Capsularis 48b

Superficial
Glutaeus 67

Internal 79c
& Ext.
Vastus 79b

Rect.
Fem. 79a

Int.
Vastus 79c

Biceps 70

Adductor Fem. 76 &
Semimembranosus 72

Gracilis 74

Obturator
Internus 77c

Piriformis 68b

Psoas
Minor
63

Rectus
Fem.79a Ilio-
Ext. Obl. Psoas
of Abd. 30a 64

Rectus
Abd. 31

Pectineus
75

Gastroc-
nemius 80

Internal
Vastus 79c

Biceps 70

Semi-
tendinosus 71

Pectineus

Capsularis
48
b

Internal Oblique
of the Abdomen 30b

Tensor Fasciae Latae 66

Ext Obl of
the Abdomen 30a

Iliacus 64b

Ischium

Middle
Glutaeus 68a

Deep
Glutaeus
69

Middle
Glutaeus

Superficial
Glutaeus 67

Capsularis 48b

External
Vastus
79b

Fl. Perforatus 86
Gastrocnemius
80

Rectus
Fem. 79a

Internal
Vastus 79c

External Vastus
79b

Popliteus 88

Peronaeus Ter. 82)
and Long
Digital Extensor
84

68

a

Superficial
Glutaeus 67

Front View of Femur and Pelvis

79b. External Vastus (V. Lateralis). Yellow. Pls. 2, 3, 7, 8, 9, 11. See 79c.

79c. Internal Vastus (V. Medialis). Green. Pls. 8, 9.

The Vasti differ from their partner, the Rectus Femoris, in that though their tendons are inserted on the knee-cap their origins are only on the femur.

Their action consequently is limited to extending the stifle joint, or of course to preventing it flexing, an office often demanded of them. They correspond to the big muscles on the top of our own thigh, which we can use to straighten our knee, or to support ourselves with our knees bent.

80a. Gastrocnemius. Blue. Pls. 2, 3, 7, 8, 9, 11.

This muscle, which corresponds to our calf, has two heads which arise on each side of the lower third of the femur. Their joint tendon, the Tendo Achillis, is attached with the Perforatus (86) to the tip of the tuber calcis of the hock.

Action: It extends the hock, or if the hock is fixed can flex the stifle; but owing to the 'parallel strings' (see 82 and 86), it cannot do both at once.

80b. Tendo Achillis. Blue. Pls. 7, 11.

See above. This name is more generally used to designate the aggregated tendons which are attached to the point of the hock.

81. *Soleus.* Red. Pls. 2, 3, 7, 9, 11.

A thin muscle from the head of the fibula, which joins the tendon of the Gastrocnemius (80).

The following muscles show a close similarity of construction to the muscles of the lower fore leg.

82. *Peronæus Tertius (Tendo-femoro-metatarseus).* Red. Pls. 7, 8, 9, 11.

This is really less a muscle than a tendinous string

which connects the bottom of the femur with the cannon bone. Its tendon splits opposite the hock joint (to allow the tendon of the Tibialis Anterior (83) to pass through), the branches of the tendon being attached to the outside of the hock joint and to the cannon bone.

Action: It flexes the hock, and indirectly the stifle (see p. 20, also the Superficial Digital Flexor (86)). It also relieves the muscles when the leg is supporting weight (see p. 14).

83. *Anterior Tibial Extensor* (*Tibialis Anterior*). Yellow. Pl. 9.

It lies on the front of the leg, running from the top of the tibia to the inside of the hock and cannon bone, having passed through and over the Peronæus Tertius (82).

Action: It flexes the hock joint.

84. *Anterior or Long Digital Extensor* (*Ext. Pedis*). Green. Pls. 2, 3, 7, 9, 11.

Its origin is on the lower end of the outside of the femur. Its tendon passes down on the front of the hock joints towards the outside, gradually sloping across the cannon bone, till it passes across the middle of the fetlock joint to be inserted on the third phalanx. A third of the distance down the cannon bone it is joined by the tendon of the Lateral Extensor (85).

Action: It extends the digits and flexes the hock joint.

85. *Lateral Digital Extensor of the Hind Leg.* Yellow. Pls. 2, 3, 7, 9.

It forms the central mass of the side of the leg. It takes its rise from the stifle joint, the tibia and the head of the fibula. Its tendon passes down the side of the hock joint to join that of the preceding muscle.

Action: To reinforce the action of the Long Digital Extensor.

86. *Superficial Digital Flexor* (*Perforatus or Plantaris muscle*). Red. Pls. 7, 8, 9, 11.

Like the Peronæus Tertius (82), it is more a tendinous string than a muscle. It starts from the femur between the two heads of the Gastrocnemius (80a), and is hidden by them until its tendon appears twisting round their tendon, so that it is on top at the tuber calcis of the hock. It forms a sort of cap over the hock on either side of which it is inserted with the tendon of the Biceps (70) and the Semitendinosus (71). Thence a broad tendon passes down the back of the leg, to which it gives its form, to be inserted on the second phalanx, as is the Perforatus (60) in the fore limb.

Action: It extends the hock automatically when the stifle joint is extended. Also, since it is continued to the foot, it flexes the digits (see p. 24).

87. *Deep Digital Flexor* (*Perforans*). Mauve. Pls. 2, 3, 7, 9, 11. This muscle is composed of three parts:

87a. the *Flexor Hallucis longus*, the deepest and strongest part, which arises from the back of the tibia and passes down the inner side of the hock in the tarsal groove;

87b. the *Tibialis posterior*, the tendon of which joins that of the preceding muscle just above the hock; and

87c. the *Long Digital Flexor*. The latter's tendon passes down the side of the hock in front of the tendon of the Flexor Hallucis longus and they unite a third of the way down the cannon bone. A check ligament, much weaker than that of the fore limb, now joins the united tendon, which passes through the ring of the preceding muscle, to be inserted within the hoof on the underside of the third phalanx, the coffin bone.

Action: It extends the hock joint and also flexes the foot (see p. 24).

88. *Popliteus.* Yellow. Pls. 8, 9.

It swings sharply across the back of the stifle joint from its origin on the outside of the femur to its insertion on the inner edge of the tibia.

Action: It helps to flex the stifle and rotates the leg inwards.

89. *The Suspensory Ligament (Interosseus medius) of the Hind Leg.* Blue. Pls. 9, 11.

As in the fore leg, it is practically only a tendon of considerable elasticity. It originates at the back of the hock and of the cannon bone, and divides into two parts which are attached to the sesamoid bones, and an extension passes forward on each side of the fetlock to join the Long Extensor (84).

Action: It supports the fetlock and prevents the pasterns from buckling over (see p. 23).

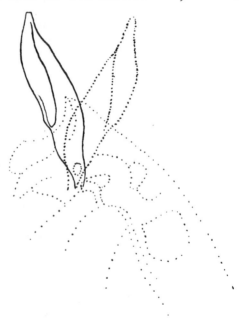

Rotation of the Ear

90. *The Ear.* Pl. 1.

The ear is a trumpet of cartilage, which carries sound to the orifice in the skull that leads to the tympanum. Its lower end is hidden by muscles and the parotid gland.

The muscles that move the ear are thin sheets that are hardly noticeable and do not much concern the artist. What does concern him is the extreme mobility of a horse's ears, which has great effect upon his expression. They are cocked when he is interested, droop when he is tired, and are laid back when he is out of temper. He moves them unceasingly to get information, as is clearly seen in a blinkered horse, whose ears are frequently turned backwards, to learn what is going on behind him. What makes them difficult to draw is that they rotate as well as rise and fall.

91. *The Eye.* Pl. 1.

The muscles of the eyebrow and surrounding parts do not concern the artist except in the changes of expression produced by their action.

The horse, like other fugitive animals, has its eyes set upon a knob on the side of the head, which allows it to look behind it by a very slight movement of the neck.

The inner corner of the eye is squarer than it is often

Plate 9. Bones and Muscles of the Hind Leg

[*The numbers printed after the names of muscles are the numbers of the other plates in which the muscles appear. The plates in which the muscles are best shown are numbered in heavier type.*]

*Numbers
and Colours
of the Muscles*

70. Red   *Biceps Femoris.* Pl. 3, 7, **8**, 11.
71. Green   *Semitendinosus.* Pl. 2, 3, 7, **8**, 11.
72. Blue   *Semimembranosus.* Pl. 2, 7, **8**, 11.
73. Mauve   *Sartorius.* Pl. **8**.
74. Yellow   *Gracilis.* Pl. **8**.
76. Mauve   *Adductor Femoris.* Pl. 7, **8**.
79a. Red   *Rectus Femoris.* Pl. 2, 3, 7, **8**, 11.
79b. Yellow   *External Vastus (V. lateralis).* Pl. 2, 3, 7, **8**, 11.
79c. Green   *Internal Vastus (V. medialis).* Pl. **8**.
80a. Blue   *Gastrocnemius.* Pl. 2, 3, 7, **8**, 11.
81. Red   *Soleus.* Pl. 2, 3, 7, 11.

*Numbers
and Colours
of the Muscles*

82. Red   *Peronaeus Tertius.* Pl. 7, **8**, 11.
83. Yellow   *Anterior Tibial Extensor.*
84. Green   *Anterior or Long Digital Extensor (Ext. pedis).* Pl. 2, 3, 7, 11.
85. Yellow   *Lateral Digital Extensor.* Pl. 2, 3, 7.
86. Red   *Superficial Digital Flexor (Perforatus or Plantaris).* Pl. 7, **8**, 11.
87. Mauve   *Deep Digital Flexor (Perforans) and check ligament.* Pl. 2, 3, 7, 11.
87c. Mauve   *Long Digital Flexor (part of 87).*
88. Yellow   *Popliteus.* Pl. **8**.
89. Blue   *Suspensory Ligament.* Pl. 11.

9

Inside

Front

Back

Outside

Rectus 79a

Ext. Vast. 79b   Gastrocnemius 80a   Lateral Digl. Extr. 85

Fr. Perforatus 86

Long Digl. Ext. 84

Biceps 70

Peronaeus Tertius 82 and Long Digl Ext

Biceps 70

Anterior Tibial 83 Extr

Popliteus 88

Lateral Extensor 85

Flexr. Perforans 87

Gastrocnemius 80a

F. Perforatus 86, Biceps 70 and Semitendinosus 71

Lateral Extensor 85

Ant. or Long Extr. 84

Suspensory Ligament 89

Long Digl. Extr. 84

Perforatus 86

Peronaeus Tertius 82

Anterior Tibial 83

Soleus 81

Gastrocnemius

Deep Flex. Perforans

Popliteus 88

F. Perforatus 86, Gastrocnemius 80a

Perforatus 86

Perforans 87

Suspensory Ligament 89

Perforatus 86

Perforans 87

Perforans 87

Gastrocnemius 80a   Semitendinosus 71 Int. Vastus 79c

Long Flexr.

Perforans

Semitendinosus 71

F. Perforatus 86

Suspensory Ligament 89

Soleus 81

Biceps 70

Long Ext. 84

Lateral Extensor 85

Rectus Fem. 79a   External Vastus 79b

Biceps 70

Knee-cap

Ant. Tib. 83

Fascia

Biceps 70

F. Perforans 87

Long Flex.

Peronaeus Tert. 82

Anterior Tibial 83

Peronaeus Tert. 82 and Ant. Tib. 83

Long Digl. Extensor 84

Suspensory Ligament 89

Long Digl. Extr. 84

Soleus 81

Fr. Perforans 87

Long Extensor 84

Anterior Tibial 83

Gastrocnemius 80a

Biceps 70

Lateral Extr. 85

Perforatus and Check Ligament 87

Perforatus 86

Perforatus 86

Perforans 87

Internal Vastus 79c   Sartorius 73   Semitendinosus 71   Gracilis 74

Popliteus 88

Long Extensor 84

Gastrocnemius 80a

Ant. Tibial Extensor 83

Peronaeus Tertius 82

Suspensory Ligament 89

Long Digl. Extr. 84

Adductor 76 and Semimembranosus 72   Internal Vastus 79c   Rectus 79a

Gracilis 74

Semitendinosus 71

Popliteus 88

Biceps 70, Semitendinosus 71 and Fr. Perforatus 86

Peronaeus Tertius 82

Anterior Tibial 83

Long Digl. Extr. 84

depicted in pictures: and the pupil in an ordinary light is not round like that of human beings, but elliptical.

92. *Veins.* Blue.

Of a horse's veins some are noticeable always, others only after exertion.

A thin-skinned horse like a thoroughbred, after it has been raced, is covered with a network of distended veins. But on all horses the following more important veins are always noticeable: the large *Facial* vein (92a), which runs along the front edge of the masseter muscle past the end of the zygomatic ridge (see Pl. 1), the *Jugular* vein (92b, see Pls. 1, 2, 3, 10), the *Cephalic* vein (92c), which runs up the inside of the fore leg along the radius, the *External Thoracic* vein (92d), which lies along the upper side of the deep pectoral muscle, under the girth (see Pls. 2, 3), the *Saphenous* vein (92e), on the inside of the femur and tibia.

Chapter V. Proportions

An anatomy book should, I suppose, mention the proportions of a horse, for they help the draughtsman to 'get it right'.

The body of a horse goes generally speaking into a square; that is, the length of the body from the point of the shoulder

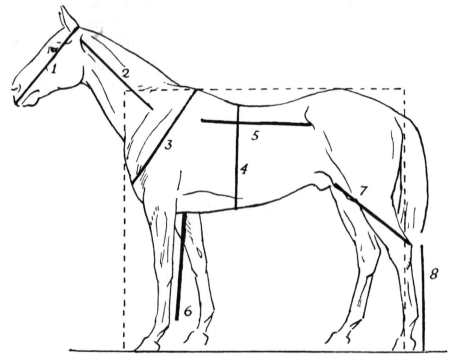

Measurements in 'Heads'

to the extremity of the haunches is approximately the height from the ground to the top of the withers.

A draught horse is generally longer than he is high: a race-horse sometimes higher than he is long. Yet Eclipse, the race-

84

horse that was never beaten, was longer by a tenth than he was high.

The head is a useful unit of measurement that corresponds *'Head'* with certain divisions of the body which are marked on the diagram.

1. The length of the head from the crest to the nose is equal to

2. The length from the wing of the atlas bone to the base of the neck.

3. The distance from the point of the shoulder to the top of the withers.

4. The depth of the body.

5. The distance from the shoulder blade to the point of the haunch (the external angle of the ilium).

6. The distance from the breast bone to just above the fet-lock.

7. The length from the stifle to the hock.

8. The distance from the hock to the ground.

Colonel Duhousset, in his book on the horse, has made out a table of a great many more measurements based on half-heads, and on dis-
tances such as that
between the mid-
dle of the hock and
the fetlock. But
they are too intri-
cate, I think, to be
really useful.

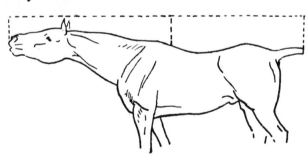

Barye, the French animal sculptor, makes the following notes about the horse.

That the length from the beginning of the mane to the tip of the lips is longer than the distance from the mane to the end of the tail. He makes a drawing something like this, the tail being docked. When the horse is not holding his head out, his body looks the longer.

He summarizes the parts of a thoroughbred thus: Four long parts: the neck, the upper bones of the leg, the belly and the haunches. Four short parts: the loins, the ears, the pasterns and the tail. Four broad parts, the forehead, the chest, the croup, the limbs. He is apparently classifying them as contrasting elements of design.

A foal's proportions are noticeably different from those of the mature horse. Short in the body and neck, and very long in the lower bones of the legs, it has to spread its fore legs to reach the ground with its mouth.

There are, of course, innumerable other differences between a foal and a horse, as there are between a child and a man. The shape of the skull and setting of the eye: the upright mane and matted tail: the short thigh bone: the large articulations so noticeable at the knee and hock. It stands too upon its toes, with upright pasterns, and has a sprightly action all its own.

The directions of the growth of the hair on the different parts of the body of a horse are very interesting. Generally downwards to shed moisture, it changes its direction according to the shape of the limbs and parts of the body; the different streams meeting in picturesque whirls and fan shapes.

The lie of the hair affects the appearance of a horse in that it influences the shape and position of the high lights as in sunshine; and affects the appearance of the horse when wet, whether from rain or from sweat. For a horse, unlike a dog, sweats through its skin and sweats itself wringing wet.

As one usually sees a horse from its own level, one only sees it in elevation, as the architects would say. Occasionally one sees a horse from above, as from the box of a coach, but how often does one sit on a coach? When one rides a horse one sees little more than its neck and ears, and a sharp perspective of its shoulders. Here instantaneous photography helps us in experience, for it gives us opportunities of becoming familiar with unusual aspects of a horse's shapes through the snapshots to be seen in the papers of horses falling at jumps, turning head over heels, and even breaking their necks.

Horse in the wet: showing lie of the hair

Chapter VI. Movement

When we come to draw the horse in movement anatomy must not stand in our way. Movement produces alterations in the appearance of form (elongations, curvatures, distortions) which are not merely subjects for curious notation, but are essential ingredients of the beauty and the rhythmic design that are created when the creature moves. A limb may appear longer or thinner or more curved than when it is at rest, which is as 'true' as is the effect of a circle produced by a bright object swung round and round in the air, or the appearance of a rapidly rotating wheel as a rim without spokes, an appearance so evident to us all, that we accept, nay demand, a rim without spokes as its proper representation. A little more subtlety of observation would make other changes of appearance equally familiar, and the artist could then use them in a picture without protest from the spectator.

There is so much misunderstanding on this question of 'truth' in art that I must touch upon it, though it has been discussed much too often.

I am not referring here to the wider truth, the truth to

imaginative conception which in the unity of some great work
of art justifies frank contradictions of fact: for instance, Ru-
bens' landscape in which shadows fall both away from and
towards the sun. I refer to the truth of observation of the
world we see—or rather the world we look at and don't see.
For most of us neither look nor trust our own eyes. And there
springs up in consequence a faith in the photograph, a belief
that it is true because it is 'scientific', for nowadays science
rather bullies us.

The instantaneous photograph, true as it is in one sense, is
quite untrue to what we see; as untrue to what we see as is the
X-ray photograph. Our eye can no more see the separate
phases of a rapid movement than it can perceive X-rays. Why
then is the artist to follow the instantaneous photographs any
more than he is to follow the X-ray photographs? Beauty is
but skin deep, says the X-ray camera, let me show you how
your wife really looks, and in your belief in scientific truth
you should complain of the ordinary portrait painter who
paints only her outside for you.

The camera, poor thing, is blind—blind to the beauties we
enjoy. When to our eyes horse and rider swing beautifully
and rhythmically across the turf, the camera records—it sees,
that is—a smudge, if its action is not rapid enough, or, if it is
successfully instantaneous, a frozen and chance attitude! It
never sees movement, for movement is seen only by an act of
memory, through recollection. You hear a tune because you
recall notes that have passed, and link notes heard at different
times with each other and with those that are sounding at the
moment: this is in fact the method by which you understand
this written sentence. And in result the human eye sees a
movement as a direction, which is why we can read descriptive gestures made in the air.

The grace of a dancer is composed of the phases which your
camera records as 'stills'. And if these 'stills' are used in series,

as in the cinematograph, your eye, seeing the succession of changing shapes, gets a sensation similar to that which it gets from nature and by means of similar impressions.

The artist cannot, like the cinematograph, use change to represent movement; he has to render it in fixed and unchanging materials. And therein lies his strength, for his purpose is not to reconstruct nature, but to express and communicate his own emotion and interest, whether his art be realistic or so abstract as not to be recognizably connected with natural appearance.

Too much importance has been attached to the camera's discoveries. The human eye frequently sees 'instantaneous' phases of movement. I still retain an impression received as a child, of a fox terrier galloping wildly after a ball. It disappeared suddenly behind a wall, leaving in my eye an 'instantaneous' image of its attitude, with its hind feet, as I noticed with some surprise, thrown forward beyond its chest. 'Instantaneous' attitudes were seen before the camera was invented. Many of the horses in the Parthenon Frieze are in attitudes very close to the camera's records, but they are woven into a wonderful rhythmic pattern. Meissonier, by patient study, saw such attitudes also and is often applauded for it; but his added knowledge did not widen his powers of expression, for, lacking rhythmic sense, he failed to notice the essential quality of the actions he observed.

A little attention will show you that your eyes are constantly receiving such instantaneous images, which generally pass unnoticed.

Instantaneous photographs are the anatomy of movement: very interesting to study, very useful for scientific purposes; to show how a bird flies that you may improve your aeroplane, or for watching the exit of the shell from the mouth of the gun; useful also to us for the better understanding of what happens in a horse's action, for such study is in its essence scientific. But to the artist an isolated instantaneous photograph is not of use in his particular kind of observation of movement, for rarely does an instantaneous photograph capture a rhythmic pattern, and it is by rhythmic pattern that movement is expressed in works of art.

But what of the ridiculous attitude accepted in old pictures? exclaims the Adversary, generally a man of science. The tub-like creatures raised on their hind legs pawing towards the sky! The outstretched racers suspended above the ground with their fore feet impossibly in front of their nose! They're just conventions, symbols without sense, consecrated by tradition!

Scientifically and factually they are wrong of course. But are they rhythmic? The appeal is to the court of art, and the touchstone of our judgment is 'truth' of impression, not truth to fact; and where the pictorial intention is the expression of movement, all fail alike, photographic image, tub-like prancer, outstretched racer that have not rhythm. Rhythmic pattern is 'true', because it is true to human visual impression; because we see rhythmic pattern as a creature moves, as the wind runs across the corn, as the water flows and ripples. And so, by fundamental association with visual experience,[1] pictorial rhythm is the true means of expressing the designs and beauty which are born only of movement.

One of the sources of our pleasure in rhythmic movement is the crescendo and diminuendo with its sense of climax, however slight; you feel it at each stride of a horse even in a flowing uninterrupted gallop.

Even simple actions have a multiplicity of rhythms of different speeds moving in different directions more intricate than those of an elaborate musical composition. Parts of a body are

[1]Possibly the associations are raised by the action of the eye, muscular or other, in following the rhythmic shapes across the surface of the picture, and following them in imagination beyond the picture plane into space. Is there possibly an alteration of focus in looking from foreground to distance in a picture, in spite of their being on the same plane, as there is in looking at near and distant objects in reality?

Rhythmic advancing, while others are receding, others stationary; parts
Pattern rise while others fall. And to add to the intricacy, objects that
are moving too fast to be visible, like the spokes of a rapidly
rotating wheel, may become visible because we are not following them with our eyes.[1] In consequence things appear curved,
distorted, elongated, and, when such alterations of appearance
are essential ingredients of the design, they must be accepted
and used.

Rhythmic pattern gives the sense of movement in a picture,
even if looked at upside down. It is a very subtle instrument,
and it can be so designed as to convey a sense of movement in
a particular direction and at a particular speed. How potent it
is is shown in a picture I have in mind. A group is represented
as pulling to the left, but they form a design of which the
rhythmic pattern, no doubt unintentionally, gives a sense of
moving to the right. Reason says one thing, but to a sensitive
spectator the pattern says the opposite, and the pattern
dominates.

Since, then, sensibility to rhythm is the source of our enjoyment, knowledge of what occurs, that is, knowledge that is
scientific in its essence, derived perhaps from camera or dis-
section, must be without arrogance, subservient to sensibility,
willing to be set aside when it interferes.

[1]See Chap. ix, p. 113.

Chapter VII. Art

'The only purpose of an artistic anatomy is to help the artist in the observation of form'. This, the opening sentence of this book, I should like now to modify, by saying that it can only really do this if it helps the artist to a greater aesthetic enjoyment of form.

For art is not an observation and report of natural appearance accurate in a scientific sense, but, like poetry, is the expression of emotional experience; poetry which is 'not less true to nature, because it is false in point of facts'. A phrase of Hazlitt's, who in his lectures on the English Poets begins by saying, 'The best general notion which I can give of poetry is that it is the natural impression of any object or event, by its vividness exciting an involuntary movement of imagination and passion, and producing through sympathy a certain modulation of the voice and sounds expressing it.'

Involuntary! Apparently artistic conception is as involuntary as really falling in love, varying like love in purity, depth, degree. It is often slight, trivial, temporary, which is perhaps why great artists are as rare as the world's great lovers; for to be either demands great passion, depth and constancy. In modern opinion the fount of a work of art is the sub-conscious. It is there that its conception occurs and the germ finds the ingredients and knowledge that it requires for its development. So, if our knowledge of anatomy is to be of artistic use, it must pass into the subconscious and suffer a change, as indeed much ordinary experience and much of our consciously acquired knowledge has already done.

Not only is the intellect not the faculty through which we

create art, music, or poetry, 'it cannot even be trusted to re-
cognize poetry when produced and may even hinder its production'.[1] The intellect's proper office in painting is in the
practical execution of a work. For as our spirit is lodged in a
material body, so poetry, music, painting must for their expression use the earthy forms of words, gut, coloured muds.
There is science in the execution of a work of art, and successful execution is the calculation of means to an end, however
automatic it may appear, however unconscious it may become
by practice. The difficulty in execution is the adjustment of
these two elements, intellect and imagination, that is, so to
control our earthy tools and media that we do not fall out of
the state of imagination and passion; otherwise the shapes,
colours, strokes or brushwork are no longer modulated into
the unity of a work of art, and our picture becomes cold-
blooded and literal.

In art, justification is by faith, there is no justification by
accuracy of fact or measurement, and our study of anatomy
must not become a measuring stick, a narrow conscience
thwarting our imagination, but must be so well understood
and digested that we use it unconsciously and deny it when
need is.

In drawing the artist feels the other side of the body while
he is drawing the side that he sees; so let our anatomy be to us
an inner eye, that we may wander in imagination beneath the
surface of the body, enjoying aesthetically the design, the
rhythms, the interplay of the parts of its mobile architecture,
and a new realm of artistic experience and enjoyment be
opened to us.

[1]A. E. Housman, *The Name and Nature of Poetry*.

Chapter VIII. Glossary

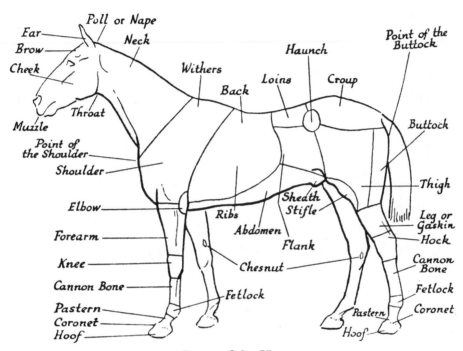

Parts of the Horse

Abdomen. The cavity of the body posterior to the diaphragm, which contains the stomach, the intestines, the liver and other organs.

Aponeurosis. A broad fibrous sheet which serves as a tendon.

Arm. A term applied to the Humerus.

Astragalus (a pulley). The bone which forms the 'wheel' of the hock joint. See Chap. II. pp. 28 and 44.

Bursa. A synovial bursa is a simple sac lubricated internally with synovial fluid, which is placed at points of pressure, as where a tendon passes over a bone.

95

Calcaneum: *Os Calcis*. Terms for the point of the hock, the heel. See Tarsus.

Cannon Bone. See Metacarpus, and Metatarsus.

Cariniform Cartilage. It may be described as the prow of the breast bone. It can be felt between the Anterior Superficial Pectoral muscles (35): see illustration of the Thorax, p. 27, Chap. II.

Carpus. The so-called 'knee' of the fore leg. It really corresponds to the human wrist and is composed of seven bones in two layers. The Pisiform bone at the back does not carry any weight, but serves as a sesamoid bone, enabling the flexors to work more efficiently. See pp. 44 and 46, and Pl. 6, p. 62.

Cartilage is gristle. It is a firm elastic substance which occurs on the end of bones, as in joints or in the prolongation of the lower ends of the ribs, being bone in a transition state. The cartilage on the top of the shoulder blade forms an elastic attachment for the muscles. See Rhomboideus (32).

Cervical Vertebræ. The seven bones of the neck. See Pl. 1, p. 12.

Cervical Ligament. The elastic cord and bands which support the head and neck. See Pl. 1, p. 12.

Chesnuts. Horny knobs which occur on the inside of the fore legs above the knee, and on the inside of the hocks. Possibly the rudiments of digits.

Coccygeal Vertebræ. They vary from fourteen to eighteen in number, from the first vertebra behind the sacrum to the last one at the tip of the tail. When a horse is docked, about six vertebræ are kept.

Coffin Bone. The third phalanx; it is hidden in the hoof.

Condyle. The term applied to the end of a bone that is somewhat cylindrical in section, forming a hinged joint, such as the elbow. *Cf*. Head of bone.

Coronet. The border or rim round the top of the hoof.

Coracoid Process. The knob at the lower end of the shoulder blade in front of the shoulder joint from which the Biceps Brachii muscle (47) arises.

Coxæ, Os Coxæ, the hip bone, which is composed of the Ilium, Ischium and Pubis. The Tuber Coxæ forms the knob of the haunch, which in a cow is so very noticeable. It is the origin of many important muscles of the hind leg.

Crest. A ridge, an elongated tubercle. The occipital crest is at the top of the skull where it joins the neck.

Croup. The upper part of the hind quarters formed by the Middle Glutæus muscle (68) and the inner angle of the Ilium. See p. 95.

Cuneiform. Wedge-shaped.

Digit. The digit consists of three phalanges (the pastern bones) and the sesamoid bones. The horse has only one digit, which corresponds to our middle finger.

Elbow. See Ulna, and Radius.

Ergot. A knob of horn situated just behind the fetlock joint, perhaps the vestige of a digit.

Extensor. A muscle that extends, opens or straightens a joint as against a flexor which closes it. In the case of the fetlock, when the foot is supporting weight the joint is 'overextended', as the pastern bones are pulled beyond the line of the cannon bone. Flexion of the fetlock consequently brings them into line with the leg before it closes the fetlock joint. Occasionally extensor and flexor muscles trespass on each other's domain.

Fascia. A sheet of connective tissue. Often, like the Fascia lata of the thigh, it acts as an aponeurosis, transmitting the pull of the muscles to the bones.

Femur. The thigh bone. It is articulated with the hip at the top; its lower end forming with the tibia and knee-cap the stifle joint.

Plate 10. Muscles of the Chest and Neck

[*The numbers printed after the names of muscles are the numbers of the other plates in which the muscles appear. The plates in which the muscles are best shown are numbered in heavier type.*]

Numbers and Colours of the Muscles

12.	Yellow	Sterno-cephalicus. Pl. 1, **2**, 3.
15*a*.	Blue	Sterno Thyro-Hyoideus.
15*b*.	Mauve	Omo-Hyoideus. Pl. 1, 2.
16*a*.	Green	Cutaneous muscle of the neck. Pl. 3.
19.	Yellow	Splenius. Pl. 1, 3.
30*a*.	Green	External Oblique of the Abdomen. Pl. 2, 3, 7, 8.
33.	Green	Latissimus Dorsi. Pl. 3, 4, 5.
34.	Red	Mastoido-Humeralis. Pl. 1, 3, 4, 5.
35.	Yellow	Anterior Superficial Pectoral. Pl. 2, 3, 5.
36.	Blue	Posterior Superficial Pectoral. Pl. 5, 6.
37.	Green	Anterior Deep Pectoral. Pl. 2, 4, 5.
38.	Red	Posterior Deep Pectoral. Pl. 2, 3, 4, 5.
41.	Blue	Supraspinatus. Pl. 2, 4.
42.	Red	Infraspinatus. Pl. 2, 4.

Numbers and Colours of the Muscles

45.	Red	Teres Major. Pl. 4.
46.	Mauve	Coraco-brachialis. Pl. 4.
47.	Green	Biceps brachii. Pl. 2, 4, 6, 11.
49.	Blue	Brachialis Anticus. Pl. 2, 3, **4**, 6.
50.	Mauve	Tensor fasciæ antibrachii. Pl. 4, 6.
51.	Yellow	Triceps Brachii. Pl. 2, 3, 4, 6, 11.
53.	Mauve	External Radial Extensor (*Ext. carpi radialis*). Pl. 2, 3, 4, **6**, 11.
54.	Green	Common Digital Extensor (*Ext. pedis*). Pl. 2, 3, 4, 6, 11.
55.	Yellow	Lateral Digital Extensor (*Ext. digiti quinti*). Pl. 2, 3, 4, 6.
59.	Blue	External Flexor of the Metacarpus (*Ext. carpi ulnaris*). Pl. 2, 3, 4, 6.
92*b*.	Blue	Jugular Vein. Pl. 1, 2, 3.

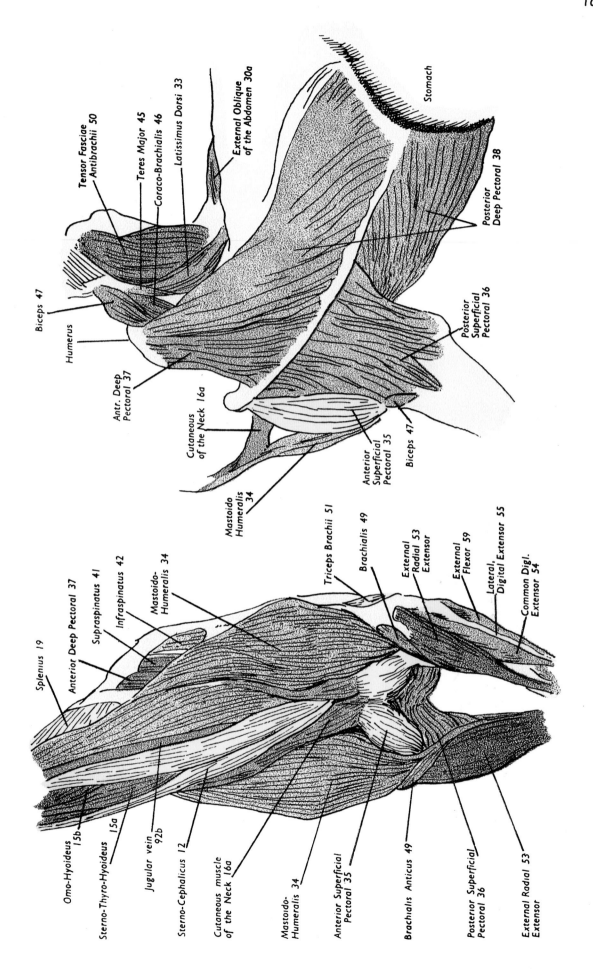

Stomach

Posterior
Deep Pectoral 38

External Oblique
of the Abdomen 30a

Latissimus Dorsi 33

Coraco-Brachialis 46

Teres Major 45

Tensor Fasciae
Antibrachii 50

Biceps 47

Humerus

Antr. Deep
Pectoral 37

Cutaneous
of the Neck 16a

Mastoido-
Humeralis
34

Anterior
Superficial
Pectoral 35

Biceps 47

Posterior
Superficial
Pectoral 36

Splenius 19

Anterior Deep Pectoral 37

Supraspinatus 41

Infraspinatus 42

Mastoido-
Humeralis 34

Triceps Brachii 51

Brachialis 49

External
Radial 53
Extensor

External
Flexor 59

Lateral,
Digital Extensor 55

Common Digl.
Extensor 54

Omo-Hyoideus
15b

Sterno-Thyro-Hyoideus
15a

Jugular vein
92b

Sterno-Cephalicus 12

Cutaneous muscle
of the Neck 16a

Mastoido-
Humeralis 34

Anterior Superficial
Pectoral 35

Brachialis Anticus 49

Posterior Superficial
Pectoral 36

External Radial 53
Extensor

Fetlock. The joint between the cannon bone (the metacarpus, or metatarsus) and the upper pastern (first phalanx); the sesamoid bones lie behind it.

Flexor. A muscle that flexes or closes a joint. See Extensor above.

Fibula. A thin bone about two-thirds of the length of the Tibia to the outer side of which it is attached.

Forearm. Its bones are the Radius, and the Ulna.

Fossa. A basin-shaped depression.

Frog. The wedge-shaped form at the back of the sole of the foot; it is formed of the most flexible horn of the whole hoof.

Gaskin. The part of the hind leg between the stifle and hock, of which the Tibia forms the bone.

Glenoid Cavity. The shallow socket at the bottom of the shoulder blade which articulates with the head of the humerus; or the groove on the skull which receives the condyle of the jaw bone.

Hand. A term of measurement; it equals four inches.

Head of a Bone. A rounded knob that forms the articulation, as opposed to a condyle which has a long bearing.

Hock. The joint on the hind leg between the stifle and the fetlock. The point of the hock is the big lever of the hind leg. See Tarsus and Calcaneus.

Hoof. The horny substance of the foot on which the horse stands. It corresponds to the nail of our third finger.

Ilium. The large bone which forms the side of the pelvic girdle. At the top it joins the sacral vertebræ forming a rigid mass with them. Its point, the Tuber Coxæ, makes the point of the haunch, and it forms with the Ischium and Pubis the cavity in which the head of the thigh bone turns.

Ischium. The end bone of the pelvis which forms the point of the buttock.

'Knee'. See Carpus.

Knee-Cap. See Patella.

Ligament. Ligaments are the binding bands which tie the bones together. The intricacy and ingenuity of their arrangement at the joints is very striking. Though flexible they are in principle inelastic. Certain ligaments are elastic, such as the Cervical ligament (11) and the Sesamoidean ligaments, which by their elasticity lift the foot as soon as it leaves the ground.

Lumbar Vertebræ. There are six just in front of the sacrum. Their transverse processes are very developed for the attachment of the strong muscles which form the shape of the loins (see illustration, p. 33, Chap. II).

Metacarpus. The large bone of the fore leg between the 'knee' and the fetlock joint. It is called the third metacarpal bone, the inside and outside splint bones attached to it being called the second and fourth metacarpals because these bones correspond to the three middle bones which form the back of the human hand, the bones of the second, third and fourth fingers, the thumb and little finger having disappeared in the horse.

Metatarsus. The cannon bone of the hind leg. The large bone between the hock and the fetlock. It is called the third metatarsal bone, the inside and outside splint bones attached to it being called the second and fourth metatarsals. These bones correspond to the three middle bones of the five which form the instep of the human foot.

Navicular Bone. A small sesamoid bone which lies behind the articulation of the second pastern and coffin bones. The Perforans Flexor (61, 87) plays over it.

'Near'. The near side of a horse is a term for the left side, the side on which a horse is usually mounted.

Occipital Bone. The highest part of the skull which articulates behind with the atlas bone.

'Off'. The off side of a horse is a term for its right side. See 'Near'.

Pastern. See Phalanx.

Patella. The knee-cap. The small bone which plays over the front of the lower end of the thigh bone (femur) to facilitate the action of the tendons that extend the stifle joint, in which it is embedded.

Phalanx, or Pastern. The three bones below the fetlock joint, which correspond to the three end joints of our middle finger.

Pisiform Bone, or Accessory Carpal. See Carpus.

Process. A general term for a prominence, more exactly a prolongation of a bone.

Pubis. The bone that forms the base of the pelvic girdle. See Ilium.

Radius. The large bone of the forearm to which the ulna is welded. These two bones in the human arm are separate, which gives us the power of turning the hand over (see p. 38).

Ribs. There are usually eighteen on each side of the horse. Articulated with the backbone at the top, they are connected by cartilage to the breast bone and each other, which gives them liberty of movement as in breathing.

Sacrum. It is a solid mass of five vertebræ to which the ilium is firmly attached.

Scapula. The shoulder blade.

Sesamoid. A term for bones that give leverage to the action of the muscles; more especially the small bones behind the pasterns which help the play of the tendons. They move backwards and forwards on the fetlock joint, being attached to the first phalanx.

Sesamoidean Ligaments. See Ligament.

Shoulder Blade. The top bone of the fore limb, the scapula.

Sinus. An air cavity in a bone, such as the large cavities in the skull, which communicate with the outer air, directly or indirectly through the nose.

Skull. Is really formed of several bones, but from the artist's point of view may be considered a unit.

Spine. Is a pointed process.

Splint Bone. See Metacarpus and Metatarsus.

Sternum. The breast bone.

Stifle. The joint between the femur and the tibia. It corresponds to our knee joint, being the true knee, which the 'knee' of the fore leg is not.

Symphysis. The union of two similar bones joined by fibrous cartilage, as the Symphysis Pubis.

Synovial sheaths and membranes are lubricated channels for the tendons, and coverings for the joints.

Tarsus, or hock, is composed of six bones. This construction gives it elasticity to meet the tremendous strains to which it is subjected. The Astragalus bone, the pulley, is the nearest approach to a wheel that we find in the construction of the horse (see pp. 28, 44).

Tendon. It is the inelastic string or band by which a muscle is attached.

Thigh. See Femur.

Thorax. The chest of the horse (see p. 27).

Tibia. The bone that lies between the stifle joint and the hock. See Fibula.

Trochanter. A name for big prominences, *e.g.* on the femur.

Trochlea. A pulley-like articulation. See for instance Tarsus.

Tuber. A large rounded projection, as Tuber Calcis, the point of the hock.

Ulna. The bone which forms the elbow. See Radius.

Vertebræ. The bones which compose the vertebral column from the top of the neck to the tip of the tail. The vertebral column is for convenience divided into the following sections:

seven cervical vertebræ of the neck; eighteen thoracic vertebræ which carry the ribs; six lumbar vertebræ which form the loins; five sacral vertebræ welded into a solid mass; sixteen coccygeal on an average, which include the tail.

Xiphoid Cartilage. The posterior tip of the sternum, it falls under the girth.

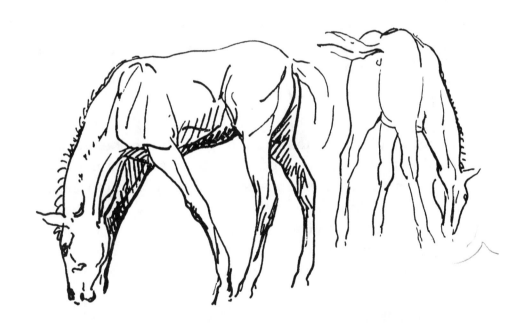

Chapter IX. Notes on the Text

From Chapter I, page 3.

Weight on Fore and Hind Limb

The proportion of a horse's weight carried by the fore feet and hind feet is approximately 5 to 4. And the fore legs also carry two-thirds of a rider's weight, if the rider is sitting back, and even more of a jockey's weight, since jockeys took to perching like monkeys on the withers, a style introduced by the successful American rider, Tod Sloan, towards the end of the nineteenth century.

The position in which the horse's head is held causes, it is stated, considerable variations in the weight carried by the fore legs. If the reader is interested to pursue the subject further he will find it discussed at length in Goubeau and Barrier's *Exterior of the Horse*.

From Chapter II, page 14.

The Jump

Instantaneous photography has made clear what really occurs in animal motion. It shows that a horse does not employ the *jump* when he gallops, as fast-running animals such as deer, hares and greyhounds do, meaning by a jump the action in which the hind legs are the last to leave the ground (1) before the period of suspension in the air (2), and the fore legs the first to meet it again (3). It is in this order that a horse employs his legs when he actually jumps, whereas he does the

opposite when he gallops; for then his fore legs are the last to *The Gallop*
leave the ground before the period of suspension, and his hind
legs the first to strike it again.

The advantage of this latter method of progression is that
only a short part of the stride is spent in suspension in the air,
the horse being supported on the ground during the rest of
his stride sometimes by two legs, sometimes by one. A stride
is the distance covered between one footfall and the next footfall of the same foot. The following is a brief statement of a
horse's gallop, which the sketches will help to explain.

After his period of suspension in the air (4) a horse lands,
let us say, on his right hind leg (5), and is supported by it
alone until he puts down his left hind
leg (6), when he advances on the two together; as the right hind leg leaves the
ground, the left hind leg is at the point

at which it passes from the position of support to that of propulsion, so at this moment he puts down the right front
leg (7) and travels on the two legs together, until at the moment
that the fore leg becomes upright, the left hind leg in its turn
leaves the ground (8). Now he is supported by the right fore
leg alone, until he puts down the other fore leg (9), when he
advances on both together up to the time of the last phase (10);

The Gallop then the right fore leg is lifted, leaving the left fore leg to finish the stride by itself and complete the projection of the horse into the air for the period of suspension, after which he lands on his right hind leg again (5), to repeat the series of movements.

The legs which made the greatest efforts were the right hind leg and the fore leg, the 'leading' leg, which was the last to leave the ground, for they in turn supported the horse without help. Therefore a rider makes his mount change from time to time the leg on which he leads, to give the legs an equal share of work.

It is because he is supported in this way, and his body travels most of the time on the same level, that a horse combines endurance so remarkably with speed. The greatest effort in animal locomotion is the throwing up and catching of the body during the period of suspension; for which reason a greyhound tires quickly, having two periods of suspension in a stride, one of them of great length.

Action of the Let us look at the sequence of a greyhound's movements,
Greyhound beginning with his longer period of suspension in the air (11).

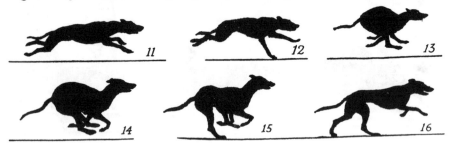

Since it is a true jump, he lands on one of his fore legs (12), quickly puts down the other fore leg and immediately, before his hind legs can reach the ground, projects himself into the air again (13) for his second and shorter period of suspension. This time his action is in principle the same as that of the horse, for it is his fore legs that have lifted his forehand into the air, and his hind legs that catch him on landing. This second period of suspension (14) is very short, however, for *Action of the* the hind legs, having been brought right in front of his fore *Greyhound* legs by the arching of the loins, take the ground almost immediately. This position, which is illustrated in sketch (13), is very characteristic of a greyhound's action. He is bent like a spring in preparation for the big jump, his longer period of suspension, which forms *half of his stride* (11). For when he lands on his hind legs after his lesser suspension he does not run smoothly, on hind legs and fore legs in sequence, as a horse does, but straightway jumps from his hind legs into the air, lifting himself a considerable height from the ground. His jumping action makes him a good sprinter, very quick off the mark, but it tires him very rapidly.

A greyhound covering ten feet in his total stride covers five feet in his 'jump' (11), two feet between the footfalls of his fore legs (12), two feet in his next suspension (14), followed by a step of a foot between his hind legs (16). Thus he is in the air with all his legs off the ground for an aggregate distance of seven feet out of the ten!

According to Muybridge, a horse striding 22 ft. 10 ins. *Period of* covers 6 ft. 6 ins. in the air (4), 3 ft. 10 ins. between his hind *Suspension* feet (6), 7 ft. 6 ins. between the hind foot and the diagonal fore foot (7), and 5 ft. between his fore feet (9). Thus he is in the air only for rather more than a quarter of his total stride. As the total stride is given as taking .44 of a second, and the period of his suspension as .088, he travels in the air at a rate that is quicker than his average rate when he is in contact with the ground, and his suspension takes only a fifth of the total time of the stride, less than one-tenth of a second. The lift required to carry him over so short a period of suspension is very small, hardly disturbing the level flow of his action.

It may make some of the action clearer if we think of the fore and hind quarters as separate units, like the two actors

Plate 11. Diagram of the Muscles of the Fore and Hind Limbs

[*The numbers printed after the names of muscles are the numbers of the other plates in which the muscles appear. The plates in which the muscles are best shown are numbered in heavier type.*]

Numbers
and Colours
of the Muscles

39*b.*   Mauve   *Serratus Thoracis.* Pl. 2, 3, 4, 5.

47.   Green   *Biceps brachii.* Pl. 2, 4, **6**, 10.

51*a.*   Yellow   *Triceps, long head.* Pl. 2, 3, 4, **6**.

51*b.*   Yellow   *Triceps, external head.* Pl. 2, 3, 4, **6**, 10.

52.   Red   *Anconeus.* Pl. 4, **6**.

53.   Mauve   *External Radial Extensor (Ext. carpiradialis).* Pl. 2, 3, 4, **6**, 10.

54.   Green   *Common Digital Extensor (Ext. pedis).* Pl. 2, 3, 4, **6**, 10.

60.   Red   *Superficial Digital Flexor (Perforatus) and check ligament,* Pl. 4, **6**.

61.   Mauve   *Deep Digital Flexor (Perforans) and check ligament.* Pl. 4, **6**.

62.   Blue   *Suspensory Ligament.* Pl. **6**.

66.   Mauve   *Tensor fasciæ latæ.* Pl. 3, **7**, 8.

68*a.*   Mauve   *Middle Glutæus.* Pl. 2, **7**, 8.

70.   Red   *Biceps Femoris.* Pl. 3, **7**, 9, 11.

71.   Green   *Semitendinosus.* Pl. 2, 3, **7**, 8, 9.

72.   Blue   *Semimembranosus.* Pl. 2, **7**, 8, 9.

79*a.*   Red   *Rectus Femoris.* Pl. 2, 3, **7**, 8, 9.

79*b.*   Yellow   *External Vastus (V. lateralis).* Pl. 2, 3, **7**, 8, 9.

80*a.*   Blue   *Gastrocnemius.* Pl. 2, 3, **7**, 8, 9.

80*b.*   Blue & Red   } *Tendo Achillis,* see *Gastrocnemius* (80*a*) p. 77.

81.   Red   *Soleus.* Pl. 2, 3, **7**, 9.

82.   Red   *Peronæus Tertius.* Pl. **7**, 8, 9.

84.   Green   *Long Digital Extensor.* Pl. 2.

86.   Red   *Superficial Digital Flexor (Perforatus).* Pl. **7**, 8, 9.

87.   Mauve   *Deep Digital Flexor (Perforans).* Pl. 2, 3, **7**, 9.

89.   Blue   *Suspensory Ligament.* Pl. 9.

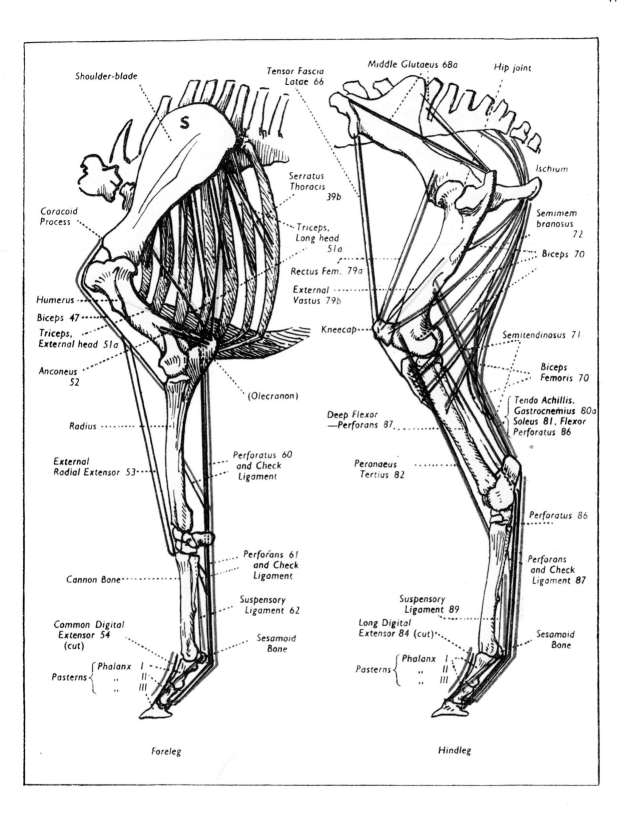

Foreleg

Hindleg

Shoulder-blade

Tensor Fascia
Latae 66

Middle Glutaeus 68a

Hip joint

S

Serratus
Thoracis
39b

Ischium

Triceps,
Long head
51a

Semimem
branosus
72

Rectus Fem. 79a

Biceps 70

Coracoid
Process

External
Vastus 79b

Kneecap

Semitendinosus 71

Humerus

Biceps 47

Triceps,
External head 51a

Anconeus
52

Biceps
Femoris 70

(Olecranon)

Deep Flexor
—Perforans 87

Tendo Achillis.
Gastrocnemius 80a
Soleus 81. Flexor
Perforatus 86

Radius

Peronaeus
Tertius 82

External
Radial Extensor 53

Perforatus 60
and Check
Ligament

Perforatus 86

Cannon Bone

Perforans 61
and Check
Ligament

Perforans
and Check
Ligament 87

Suspensory
Ligament 62

Suspensory
Ligament 89

Common Digital
Extensor 54
(cut)

Long Digital
Extensor 84 (cut)

Sesamoid
Bone

Sesamoid
Bone

Pasterns { Phalanx I
,, II
,, III

Pasterns { Phalanx I
,, II
,, III

concealed in the stage donkey, though, of course, more closely *Jump and* coupled and interdependent. *Gallop*

In a trot the partners run with opposite legs. Bill's right leg to Tom's left, Bill's left to Tom's right. It is the smoothest way for two men to carry anything.

In a gallop Bill and Tom act at different times, Tom the hind quarters leaping first, Bill stepping out widely as he feels Tom catching him up, leaping in his turn before Tom has returned to the ground, so that for a moment they are both in the air together. Their movements represent a horse's action very closely, for a horse's fore legs hurry, just as Bill did, when the quarters, thrown up and forward with added momentum, press forwards on to them. Photography and the position of his footfalls show that at each stride the fore feet take a considerably wider step than do the hind feet. Thus, in a gallop, as opposed to a jump, it is apparently the fore legs which undertake the accelerated propulsion of the forehand. In a jump, or the long period of suspension of a greyhound's action, the fore legs, when raising the forehand, cannot really add to its acceleration, as they must conform to the speed of the hind quarters, which are in the air or just taking the ground; thus the forehand has to wait in the air for the thrust of the hind quarters to add to its acceleration. Bill, that is, jumps into the air and Tom propels Bill's weight as well as his own.

The advantage of a horse's method of galloping is that both fore and hind legs share in the duties of supporting and propelling the body.

The stiffness of the construction of a horse's back and loins, which suits his action, as a greyhound's suppleness suits his undulating leaps, makes it possible for a horse to carry the weight of a rider.

The action of a canter is similar to that of a gallop, in that *The Canter* the horse on landing after suspension is on one hind leg and before suspension on one fore, but it differs in that he has at times three legs on the ground, which never occurs in a gallop. The slower the pace the greater the need for support.

The Trot   In a trot each fore foot, with a diagonal hind foot, is lifted alternately; the horse being, in a fast trot, twice off the ground in a stride. As it is a very level motion, the horse can keep up a trot for a long while.

The Walk   In a walk, as it is the slowest pace, a horse requires a great amount of support, and is on three legs and two alternately; in a very slow walk he lifts only one leg at a time, having always three and sometimes even four feet on the ground.

Monsieur Marey, by an apparatus attached to a horse's feet, plotted exactly the time that each foot was on the ground in the different paces. Some of his diagrams are given in Goubeau and Barrier's *Exterior of the Horse*, if the reader wishes to pursue the subject. I think the artist is better employed in watching the paces and seeing what they *look like to him*.

From Chapter II, page 16.

Leg v.   It is because it is lifted at every stride that the leg has this
Wheel   freedom of movement, thereby gaining an advantage over the wheel; for the principle of altering their relative positions cannot be applied between the hub of a wheel and the body of a car, since the propulsive agent, the driving wheel, is uninterruptedly in contact with the ground.

From Chapter II, page 19.

Horse-Power   Horse-power: 'H.P.' is so familiarly used nowadays in relation to motor cars that it is interesting to learn that a horse, a vague enough term, can develop 27 h.p.

In America they have competitions, which, it is stated, excite enormous interest, to test the power of draught horses. A 'Tractor Dynamometer' is used, to which the horses are harnessed. It records the total power exerted by a team of horses and also that of each member of the team.

It is argued that draught-horse breeding has not made the *Horse-Power* same progress as racehorse breeding because the dams and sires are not chosen for actual performance. Racehorses are

selected for stud on their known qualities of speed, endurance, etc., these being judged on the recorded performances of themselves and their forbears. Draught horses have been selected on the opinion of judges upon their conformation, without the corrective of competition and the tests that such a machine would give.

From Chapter II, p. 21.

The action of these muscles is a good instance of how diverse the applications of the force of a single muscle can be.

The Biceps femoris (70), for instance, has four points of attachment (see Pls. 8, 11) originating from the rump and buttock: it is inserted (*a*) on the back of the femur; (*b*) on the knee-cap; (*c*) on the tibia; and (*d*) sends a tendon to the hock.

Multiple Action of a Muscle

Biceps Femoris
(a, b, c, c', d)
shown thus _____

Semitendinosus
shown thus _ _ _ _ _ _ _

Though at first sight its pull at these various points may appear contradictory, they really all contribute to the extension of the hind leg; starting with the foot as our fixed point we see that the tendon (*d*) by pulling on the hock extends the tibia on the cannon bone ; next (c, c^1) pulling the tibia, and (b) pulling the knee-cap towards the buttock, extends the stifle joint and also extends the hip joint; (a) by pulling back the femur extends the hip joint only.

Thus the Biceps femoris, acting by itself, can extend all the joints of the hind leg simultaneously.

The Semitendinosus (71), though less complex than the preceding muscle, extends hock, stifle and hip joints simultaneously. Its insertions on the crest and the, fascia of the tibia act like sections c, c^1 of the Biceps, and its tendon to the hock acts like the Biceps' tendon (d).

From Chapter II, page 26.

Rise and Fall of Fetlock

The wheel does not have to deal with the 'crutch' or 'broomstick' difficulty, since its 'legs', the spokes, tread, so to

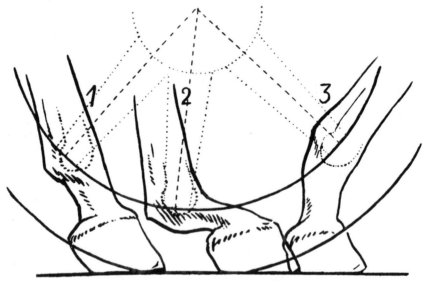

speak, on the rim and so maintain the axle always at the same height above the ground.

In the first sketch three positions of the lower end of the cannon bone and of the tip of a spoke are compared with each other, the rise and fall of the cannon bone in relation to the ground being effected by the play of the pasterns, as the rise and fall of the spoke is by the curvature of the wheel.

For illustration's sake the hoof is drawn in three different positions on the ground, which of course do not occur in a single stride; the movements of the pasterns and fetlock joints really take place over a stationary hoof as in the second sketch.

From Chapter VI, page 92.

I mention this to test your powers of observation. The phenomenon is offered you every time you are among wheeled traffic.

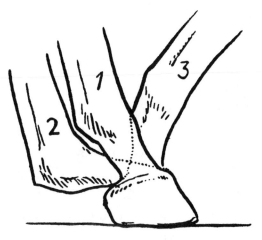

Visibility of Wheel Spokes

I am not referring to the momentary visibility of the wheels of a passing car, which, I think, everyone must have noticed, which is due to a sudden movement of your head, and is explained as follows. When you *follow* a car with your eyes, the image of the wheel is held continuously on the same part of the retina, so that the visual impressions received from the spokes are superimposed on the after images of previous impressions, resulting in a blur. If your head is suddenly displaced by a jerk (the shock of the impact of your foot upon the ground is often sufficient), the image of the wheel is transferred to a fresh part of the retina, which being free of its after images gives an 'instantaneous photograph' of the wheel with its spokes clearly separate, to be followed immediately by the normal impression of blur.

The particular phenomenon to which I referred, as a test for your powers of observation, is as follows, and I shall be surprised if you have noticed it.

Visibility of
Spokes

When a car or bicycle is approaching fix your eyes upon some point on the road near its course, selecting the spot so that the vehicle will pass within your field of vision. To keep your eyes steadily on the road may need some determination, but if you succeed you will see the spokes quite distinctly at the bottom of the wheel. They may appear curved, or even to criss-cross a little, there are variations of appearance due to difference of speed and other factors, but you will see the spokes distinctly, even spokes as thin as those of bicycles.

Above the hub I have not seen them. This is not due, I think, to their being lost by coming against the body of the car, for the spokes of bicycle wheels, which have the same background above the hub as below it, are not visible at the top.

The invisibility of spokes at the top is due to the cycloid movement of the wheel, which causes its upper half to advance —not rotate—more rapidly than the lower half which is in contact with the road.

Another effect caused by the cycloid movement is that the rim of the wheel appears as if flattened along the road some-what like the sketch, and if seen more from above like the second sketch. These appearances are not due to any  actual flattening of a pneumatic tyre, for they are equally noticeable with the iron tyre of a horse-drawn vehicle.

As we have gone so far, it may be interesting to seek the cause of these appearances.

Since the eye is fixedly watching a spot on the road, the car crosses our visual field, and blurring, due to the superposition of images, is eliminated, because the wheel is continually seen by fresh parts of the retina.

It has been suggested to me that the above explanation is probably incorrect, since it is so difficult for the human eye

not to follow moving objects, that it is almost certain that *Visibility of*
one's eyes do follow the car. Without going into detail, let me *Spokes*
say that this is not convincing, as the phenomenon may be
seen simultaneously in vehicles going opposite ways!

If the experimenter finds great difficulty in perceiving these
appearances, it is possibly due to his being untrained to pay
attention to visual impressions received near the periphery of
his retina, to his being unable consciously to notice what his
eyes offer him, which is, I think, one of the faculties which
make the artist. At any rate by this experiment he can test his
power of observation, and if successful realize how habitually
one can fail to see what one's eyes are continually reporting.
Which discovery should persuade him to trust the artist more,
when he shows him effects that he finds unfamiliar, and may
lead him to discover for himself, that many of the curvatures,
elongations, distortions of appearance caused by movement are
as essential a part of its interest and beauty, as is the apparent
alteration of a colour according to the colours that surround
and contrast with it.

Bibliography

The Head and Neck of the Horse, by O. Charnock Bradley. W. Green & Son, Edinburgh.

The Limbs of the Horse, by the same author.

The Anatomy of the Domestic Animals, by Septimus Sisson. W. B. Saunders.

The Exterior of the Horse, by Goubeau and Barrier.

The Horse in Motion, by J. D. B. Stillman. Osgood.

Points of the Racehorse, by Major-General Sir John Hills. Wm. Blackwood.

The Horse: A Guide to its Anatomy, by Ellenberger, Baum and Dittrich.

Atlas der Anatomie des Pferdes, by Schmaltz.

Index

Addenda

Chapter I. The Frame

The Frame Support of the Body (page 2)

1. Suspension of the body between the fore limbs is now recognised as being achieved by numerous muscular and tendinous attachments to the ribs vertebrae and sternum from the scapula and humerus.

2. It must also be understood that the absorption of the forces which are met when a horse lands over a jump is a function of many structures in the limb, such as the joints and their ligamentous and muscular attachments as well as the large muscle masses of the upper limb through which the concussion (now called axial compression force) is transmitted to the trunk.

The Feet (page 3)

The front feet are now estimated to carry sixty per cent of the horse's weight. This in fact is increased at the point of landing from a jump to many times the horse's bodyweight.

The Vertebral Column (page 5)

1. The union of the last lumbar vertebra to the sacrum is one which allows a considerable degree of movement, being the main pivotal joint of the back. However, movement within the almost rigid thoracolumbar region occurs between individual thoracic vertebrae, between the last thoracic and first lumbar, between the first three lumbar as well as the lumbosacral junction mentioned above. The degree of this movement is necessarily limited but overall movement in this region is given as 15 – 20cm (6 – 8 inches) for the full length of the fixed part of the spine.

2. The junction of the sacrum and the ilium, the sacroiliac joint, is also significant, as an area that encounters frequent injury in ridden and jumping horses as well as influencing the contours of surface anatomy.

127

The Neck (page 6)

Sideways movement of the head and neck allows the horse to reach its shoulder and flank and also to scratch areas such as the outer part of the hindquarter.

The Ribs (page 7)

Our present understanding is that the body is suspended from the shoulder by tendons and muscles (including the rhomboideus, trapezius and pectorals) aside from the serratus muscle. However, a significant part of the burden is borne by this muscle.

The Shoulder Blades (page 8)

The idea of the limb being brought to the centre line of motion does not apply at slow paces like the walk and trot but is an important factor in movement at faster paces.

Chapter II. Action and Mechanics

Automatic Support (page 10)

1. The automatic support that allows a horse to rest while standing is a mechanism that finds its origins in time. The primitive horse in the wild state, constantly hunted by predators, needed this facility to allow for quick escape, just as the design of his eye allowed for the visualisation of objects both far and near, and the set of the eyes allowed for a certain amount of rear vision.

The physical support mechanism, today referred to as the stay apparatus, consists of a series of tendons, ligaments and muscles which take the weight of the animal both fore and hind by locking the main joints and holding them locked until choosing to unlock them. One of the principal structures of this apparatus is the suspensory system of both fore and hind limbs. Also significant are the check ligaments, which help to relieve the main muscle bodies of the burden of weight-bearing at rest.

In the hind limb, the stay apparatus functions when the patella is locked onto the medial trochlear ridge of the femur. This is not something that can happen in both hind limbs at the same time, thus the alternating weight-bearing of these limbs. The fore limbs do not have the same impediment when resting and are able to rest together. The horse, in order to take quickly to flight, has only to unlock the patella by contraction of the quadriceps, biceps and possibly tensor fasciae latae muscles and push off. The locking of the fore limbs in this situation may well be dependent on the locking of the elbow joint, achieved by a combination of muscle and ligamentous action. It may also be significant that the extension of the weight-bearing hind limb throws more weight forwards, thus increasing this effect.

The diagrams in Plate 11 describe in fine detail virtually all structures involved in the stay apparatus of both fore and hind limbs. What these diagrams effectively mean is that the weight of the animal at rest is borne, not by the elastic skeletal musculature but by tendinous elements of particular muscles, which help to lock the limbs in such a way that the joints are stable and weight is borne down through solid bone without any natural tendency to collapse in sleep. This status is maintained on a three-limb support with alternating locking of the hind limbs being the only variable.

2. It is also important to appreciate that limb structures often play complex rather than simple parts, that a particular function, such as support of a joint, may well be the consequence of several intimate and remote structures acting together, rather than a single anatomical entity acting alone. Thus the closing of the knee and its support is facilitated by the lacertus fibrosus, but the full support of the knee is also aided by the construction of the joint, the ligaments that surround it and the tendons at both front and back. Support of the fetlock joint (preventing it from knuckling forward) is a function of the suspensory apparatus, also other tendons and their muscular bodies. This support is often lost on heavy sedation, proving that the mechanical influence of the suspensory system is not alone in this, as is pointed out later in this book.

The Back Tendons (page 21)

1. Modern concepts of fetlock construction and movement recognise attachment of the main part of the suspensory branches to the abaxial side of the sesamoid bones, meaning the ligament does not move over the joint, but moves as an integral part of a tightly bound structure, the joint over-extending as weight is borne and lowered towards the ground as this is achieved.

The sesamoidean ligaments (as many as nine in number), which bind the sesamoid bones to the fetlock, pastern and to each other, are an integral part of this.

2. It must not be forgotten that in raising the forehand, the horse also uses the powerful muscles of the back, viz the longissimus, etc.

Swing of the Pelvis (page 25)

When discerning the swing of the pelvis in the moving horse it is useful to remember that this movement only occurs at the walk and trot. At faster paces the spine is strongly supported by muscular action and saved from injuries that might ensue from this type of movement at speed.

Clearance of the Foot (page 27)

The element of increasing speed effects the manner in which the limbs advance. At walk and trot, the base of support is square, the limbs bearing weight in the same position as they stand anatomically to the body. It is at faster paces that the tendency towards a central line of support becomes evident, the hoof-prints at the gallop being closest to a straight line.

Chapter III. The Skeleton

The Neck (page 36)

1. Movement of intervertebral joints is limited in many ways by the nature and design of the specific joint, and is also complicated by the presence of intervertebral cartilaginous discs. The purpose of design is always to protect the integrity of the spine, including its vital contents (spinal cord), while still allowing for essential movement. This movement does not restrict itself to ambulation but also allows such critical acts as eating and scratching. The impression overall has to be one of strength, and although the horse suffers from back problems as a common feature of his life, fracture of vertebrae or complete dislocation are infrequently seen.

2. While the outline of the neck does not highlight the bony vertebrae, these are felt easily beneath the skin and their form is an essential landmark of surface anatomy.

The Sesamoids (page 41)

The dictionary definition of the term 'sesamoid bone' is of a small bone embedded in a tendon or joint capsule. The purpose of such a bone, as is stated in this book, is to increase the mechanical advantage at which muscles and tendons work over the particular joint. The bones we now classify as sesamoid bones are: the two proximal sesamoids of each fetlock; the distal sesamoid, or navicular bone, in the foot; the patella of the stifle; the accessory carpal of the knee. The calcaneus of the hock, because of its position and purpose, might also sit close to this classification.

Chapter IV. The Muscles

In defining muscle today, we distinguish between cardiac muscle (in the heart), smooth muscle (located in organs such as the bowel) and skeletal muscle (less commonly referred to as striated muscle now). Skeletal muscle is divided into red and white fibre types, the distinction being the function of the individual muscle, be this for speed or strength, for running or lifting, for sprinting or staying.

Description of the Muscles (page 52)

In recent times, muscle names have been standardised and books such as *Nomina Anatomica Veterinaria* were designed to set guidelines which could be used universally. This meant that those dealing with animal anatomy had a common structure to follow, whatever their purpose. Different bodies would no longer have different names for the same muscle, bone, organ, etc.

In giving herewith the modern name for each anatomical structure listed in this chapter, it has to be appreciated that current use is a fickle creature and the definitions provided by Lowes Dalbiac Luard were as correct in their time as these are today. It is not impossible that another sixty years will see changes again.

In providing the following list, the names given in the original edition are used as before. Following a hyphen, the modern common name is given with the current scientific (Latin) name provided in brackets. The term 'name unchanged' merely alludes to the common name.

Descriptive List of Muscles (page 55)

1. *Orbicular of the Mouth (Orbicularis oris)* – name unchanged (*m. orbicularis oris*).

2. *Levator of the Upper Lip and Nostril (L. nasi labialis)* – levator nasolabialis (*m. nasolabialis*).

3. *Levator of the Upper Lip (L. labii superioris proprius)* – name unchanged (*m. levator labii superioris*).

4. *Zygomaticus* – name unchanged (*m. zygomaticus*).

5. *Depressor of the Lower Lip (D. labii inferioris)* – name unchanged (*m. depressor labii inferioris*).

6. *Buccinator* – name unchanged (*m. buccinator*).

7. Masseter - name unchanged (*m. masseter*).

8. *Lateral Dilator of the Nose (Caninus muscle)* – name unchanged
(*m. caninus*).

9. *Superior Dilator of the Nose* – now classified as dorsal part of the
lateral dilator.

10. *Transverse Dilator of the Nose* – dilator of nostril (*m. dilator naris
apicalis*).

11. *Cervical Ligament (Ligamentum Nuchae)* – nuchal ligament
(*ligamentum nuchae*).

12. *Sterno-Cephalicus (Sterno-Mandibularis)* – sternocephalic
(*m. sternocephalicus*).

13. *Longus Colli* – long muscle of the neck (*m. longus colli*).

14. *Intertransversales Colli* – intertransverse (*m. intertransversarii dorsales*
and *ventrales cervicis*).

15a. *Sterno-Thyro-Hyoideus* – sternothyrohyoid (*m. sternohyoideus* and
m. sternothyroideus).

15b. *Omo-Hyoideus* – omohyoid (*m. omohyoideus*).

16. *Cutaneous Muscle (Panniculus Carnosus)* – name unchanged.

16a. *Cutaneous of the Neck* – (*m. cutaneous colli*).

16b. *Cutaneous of the Abdomen* – (*m. cutaneous trunci*).

17. *Rectus Capitis (Anticus Major)* – long muscle of the head (*m. longus
capitis*).

18a. *Trapezius Cervical part* – name unchanged (*m. trapezius*).

18b. *Trapezius Dorsal or Thoracic part* – name unchanged (*m. trapezius*).

19. *Splenius* – name unchanged (*m. splenius capitis/cervicis*).

20. *Longissimus Capitis et Atlantis* – names unchanged (*m. longissimus
capitis/atlantis*).

21. *Complexus* – name unchanged (*m. complexus*).

22. *Multifidus Cervicis* (Transverse Spinous Muscle of the Neck) –
multifidi (*mm. multifidi*).

23. *Posterior Oblique of the Head* – caudal oblique muscle of the head
(*m. obliquus capitis caudalis*).

24. *Anterior Oblique of the Head* – cranial oblique muscle of the head *(m. obliquus capitis cranialis).*

25a. *Serratus Posterior (S. Exspiratorius)* – serratus caudalis *(m. serratus dorsalis caudalis).*

25b. *External Intercostals* – name unchanged *(mm. intercostales externi).*

26. *Transversalis Costarum (Ilio-costalis)* – iliocostal *(m. iliocostalis).*

27. *Longissimus Dorsi* – longissimus *(m. longissimus).*

27a. *Spinalis* – name unchanged *(m. spinalis).*

28. *Multifidus Dorsi* – multifidi *(mm. multifidi).*

29. *The Abdominal Tunic* – name unchanged *(tunica flava abdominis).*

30a. *External Oblique of the Abdomen* – external abdominal oblique *(m. obliquus externus abdominis).*

30b. *Internal Oblique of the Abdomen* – internal abdominal oblique *(m. obliquus internus abdominis).*

31. *Rectus Abdominis* – name unchanged *(m. rectus abdominis).*

32. *Rhomboideus (Cervicalis and Thoracalis)* – rhomboids *(m. rhomboideus thoracis/cervicis/capitis).*

33. *Latissimus Dorsi* – name unchanged *(m. latissisimus dorsi).*

34. *Mastoido-humeralis* (or Brachio-cephalicus) – brachiocephalic *(m. brachiocephalicus).*

35. *Anterior Superficial Pectoral* (or *Pectoralis descendens*) – superficial pectorals *(mm. pectorales superficiales).*

36. *Posterior Superficial Pectoral* (or *Pectoralis transversus*) – superficial pectoral *(mm. pectorales superficiales).*

37. *Anterior Deep Pectoral (Sterno praescapularis)* – deep pectoral *(m. pectoralis profundus)* (sometimes called the pars scapularis).

38. *Posterior Deep Pectoral (Pectoralis ascendens)* – deep pectoral *(m. pectoralis profundus)* (sometimes called the pars humeralis).

39a. *Serratus Cervicis* – ventral serrate *(m. serratus ventralis cervicis).*

39b. *Serratus Thoracis* – ventral serrate *(m. serratus ventralis thoracis).*

40. *Deltoid* – name unchanged *(m. deltoideus).*

41. *Supraspinatus* – name unchanged *(m. supraspinatus)*.

42. *Infraspinatus* – name unchanged *(m. infraspinatus)*.

43. *Teres Minor* – name unchanged *(m. teres minor)*.

44. *Subscapularis* – subscapular *(m. subscapularis)*.

45. *Teres Major* – name unchanged *(m. teres major)*.

46. *Coraco-brachialis* – coracobrachial *(m. coracobrachialis)*.

47. *Biceps Brachii (Coraco-Radialis)* – biceps *(m. biceps brachii)*.

48a. *Capsularis Brachii* – articular muscle of the shoulder *(m. articularis humeri)*.

48b. *Capsularis Femoris* – articular muscle of the hip *(m. articularis coxae)*.

49. *Brachialis Anticus* – brachialis *(m. brachialis)*.

50. *Tensor Fasciae Antibrachii* – tensor of the antibrachial fascia *(m. tensor fasciae antebrachii)*.

51. *Triceps Brachii* – name unchanged *(m. triceps brachii)*.

51a. *Long Head (Caput Longum)* – name unchanged *(m. triceps brachii, caput longum)*.

51b. *External Head (Caput Laterale)* – name unchanged *(m. triceps brachii, caput laterale)*.

51c. *Internal Head (Caput Mediale)* – name unchanged *(m. triceps brachii, caput mediale)*.

52. *Anconeus* – name unchanged *(m. anconeus)*.

53. *External Radial Extensor (Extensor Carpi Radialis)* – radial extensor of the carpus *(m. extensor carpi radialis)*.

54. *Common Digital Extensor of the Fore Leg (Ext. Pedis)* – common digital extensor *(m. extensor digitorum communis)*.

55. *Lateral Digital Extensor (Extensor Digiti Quinti)* – name unchanged *(m. extensor digitorum lateralis)*.

56. *Oblique Extensor of the Metacarpus (Abductor Pollicis)* – oblique extensor (of carpus) *(m. abductor digiti (pollicis) longus)*.

57. *Internal Radial Flexor (Fx. Carpi Radialis)* – radial flexor of the carpus *(m. flexor carpi radialis)*.

58. *Middle Flexor of the Metacarpus (Fx. Carpi Ulnaris)* – ulnar flexor of the carpus *(m. flexor carpi ulnaris).*

59. *External Flexor of the Metacarpus (Ulnaris Lateralis)* – name unchanged *(m. extensor carpi ulnaris).*

60. *Superficial Digital Flexor (or Perforatus)* – name unchanged *(m. flexor digitorum superficialis).*

61. *Deep Digital Flexor (or Perforans) of the Fore Leg* – name unchanged *(m. flexor digitorum profundus).*

62. *The Suspensory Ligament (Interosseus Medius) of the Fore Leg* – name unchanged *(mm. interossei).*

63. *Psoas Minor* – name unchanged *(m. psoas minor).*

64. *Ilio-Psoas* – name unchanged *(m. iliopsoas).*

64a. *Psoas Major* – name unchanged *(m. psoas major).*

64b. *Iliacus* – name unchanged *(m. iliacus).*

65. *Quadratus Lumborum* – name unchanged *(m. quadratus lumborum).*

66. *Tensor Fasciae Latae* – name unchanged *(m. tensor fasciae latae).*

67. *Superficial Glutaeus* – superficial gluteal *(m. gluteus superficialis).*

68a. *Middle Glutaeus (Glutaeus Medius)* – middle gluteal *(m. gluteus medius).*

68b. *Piriformis* – name unchanged *(m. piriformis).*

69. *Deep Glutaeus* – deep gluteal *(m. gluteus profundus).*

70. *Biceps Femoris* – name unchanged *(m. biceps femoris).*

71. *Semitendinosus* – name unchanged *(m. semitendinosus).*

72. *Semimembranosus* – name unchanged *(m. semimembranosus).*

73. *Sartorius* – name unchanged *(m. sartorius).*

74. *Gracilis* – name unchanged *(m. gracilis).*

75. *Pectineus* – name unchanged *(m. pectineus).*

76. *Adductor Femoris* – adductor *(m. adductor).*

77a. *Quadratus Femoris* – name unchanged *(m. quadratus femoris).*

77b. *Obturator, Externus* – name unchanged *(m. obturatorius externus).*

77c. *Obturator, Internus* – name unchanged *(m. obturatorius internus).*

78. *Gemelli* – name unchanged *(mm. gemelli).*

79. *Quadriceps Femoris* – name unchanged *(m. quadriceps femoris).*

79a. *Rectus Femoris* – name unchanged *(m. rectus femoris).*

79b. *External Vastus (V. Lateralis)* – lateral vastus *(m. vastus lateralis).*

79c. *Internal Vastus (V. Medialis)* – medial vastus *(m. vastus medialis).*

80a. *Gastrocnemius* – name unchanged *(m. gastrocnemius).*

80b. *Tendo Achillis* – name unchanged *(tendo Achillis).*

81. *Soleus* – name unchanged *(m. soleus).*

82. *Peronaeus Tertius (Tendo-femoro-metatarseus)* – name unchanged *(m. peroneus tertius).*

83. *Anterior Tibial Extensor (Tibialis Anterior)* – cranial tibial *(m. tibialis cranialis).*

84. *Anterior or Long Digital Extensor (Ext. Pedis)* – name unchanged *(m. extensor digitorum longus).*

85. *Lateral Digital Extensor of the Hind Leg* – name unchanged *(m. extensor digitorum lateralis).*

86. *Superficial Digital Flexor (Perforatus or Plantaris Muscle)* – name unchanged *(m. flexor digitorum superficialis).*

87. *Deep Digital Flexor (Perforans)* – name unchanged *(mm. flexores digitorum profundus).*

87a. *Flexor Hallucis Longus* – lateral digital flexor *(m. flexor digitorum lateralis).*

87b. *Tibialis Posterior* – caudal tibial *(m. tibialis caudalis).*

87c. *Long Digital Flexor* – medial digital flexor *(m. flexor digitorum medialis).*

88. *Popliteus* – name unchanged *(m. popliteus).*

89. *The Suspensory Ligament (Interosseus Medius) of the Hind Leg* – interosseus *(mm. interosei).*

Addenda
Chapter V. Proportions

Growth of the Hair (page 86)

The significance of hair patterns is considered so important today that they provide the basis for identification under most breed societies. Whorls, feathering and other unusual marks (like prophet's thumb marks) are unique to the individual animal and collectively amount to the equivalent of a set of fingerprints.

Chapter VIII. Glossary

Slight changes have occurred in the common usage of bone nomenclature used in the original text:

Astragalus
The talus is the correct name for the astragalus, also known as the tibial tarsal bone.

Calcaneum
The calcaneus is now the correct name for the os calcis, also called the fibular tarsal bone.

Digit
The bones of the digit are referred to as first, second and third phalanx. The third phalanx (also called the pedal bone) is seldom called the coffin bone now, though the joint it forms with the second phalanx and the distal sesamoid (or navicular bone) is often referred to as the coffin joint.

Navicular Bone
The navicular bone is called the distal sesamoid.

Pisiform Bone
The pisiform bone at the back of the knee is now referred to as the accessory carpal.